Susan Gaum

Celebrating
FOOD

SUSAN GAUEN

CREATION
HOUSE
A STRANG COMPANY

CELEBRATING FOOD by Susan Gauen
Published by Creation House
A Strang Company
600 Rinehart Road
Lake Mary, Florida 32746
www.strangbookgroup.com

This book is not intended to provide medical advice or to take the place of medical advice and treatment from your personal physician. Readers are advised to consult their own doctors or other qualified health professionals regarding the treatment of their medical problems. Neither the publisher nor the author takes any responsibility for any possible consequences from following the information in this book.

Design Director: Bill Johnson
Cover design by Amanda Potter
Interior design by Candace Ziegler

Library of Congress Control Number: 2009932988
International Standard Book Number: 978-1-59979-890-5

First Edition

09 10 11 12 13 — 9 8 7 6 5 4 3 2 1
Printed in the United States of America

CONTENTS

PART ONE

PART TWO

PART THREE

PART FOUR

PART FIVE

PART SIX

PART SEVEN

PART EIGHT

PART NINE

PART TEN

PREFACE

Thanks to my mom, I've loved cooking since I was about eight years old. And since I'm a missionary who has lived in many different countries, having to substitute ingredients is just a normal part of my cooking experience. When my friend Tonya developed allergies to gluten, dairy, egg yolks, soy products, and some seeds, I knew I could find ways to recreate old favorites into allergy-friendly versions that she and her family could enjoy. Writing a cookbook was the last thing on my mind, but when I had such fabulous results preparing allergy-friendly foods, Tonya came up with the idea that I should write my own cookbook. Many, many hours, days, and months later, here it is!

I had several goals in mind when creating these recipes. First, I wanted to provide allergy-friendly recipes that were totally fabulous so people with food allergies could celebrate food again! Second, I wanted to save people money by offering recipes for baking mixes, instant oatmeal, rice dishes, pasta dishes, and chicken and beef dinners that could quickly and easily be made from scratch, as an alternative to the expensive store-bought versions. Third, I wanted to make recipes that were easy to make so busy moms and career people could quickly prepare allergy-friendly foods. And fourth, I wanted to make recipes that people could easily adapt to fit whatever allergies they have or don't have. It's easy to suit my recipes to any food allergy.

I hope using this cookbook will result in great meal times and save you time and money as you prepare delicious, healthy, and easy-to-make food in your own kitchen for your family and friends to enjoy!

CELEBRATING FOOD!® BAKING MIXES

All of the gluten-free baking recipes in this book were specifically formulated to be used with my two versatile and easy-to-use baking mixes: Celebrating Food!® Pancake & Baking Mix and Celebrating Food!® Pizza Crust & Yeast Bread Mix. For information about how purchase the prepared mixes online, visit www.celebratingfoodglutenfree.com.

I have also included recipes for both mixes in the book. When the recipes are carefully followed, the mixes produce moist and flavorful baked goods that will make you proud every time. Experimenting with these recipes has been a total joy for me, as well as for those who got to sample the end results! While using my baking mixes with the recipes in this book, you will be able to produce the same fabulous results for your own family and friends. It's easy!

ACKNOWLEDGMENTS

I wholeheartedly share credit for this book with all the people who came up with the idea of the book in the first place, provided me with kitchens to cook in, let me use their dishes and decorations for all my photos, and encouraged me along the way.

The project began in mid-May 2008 in Hood River, Oregon, when Tonya Dehart asked me to make this book. About one and one-half years before that, when she discovered she had multiple food allergies, I saw the many difficulties she faced trying to find foods she could eat. Tonya introduced me to gluten-free flour, egg-free mayonnaise, allergy-free chocolate chips, and many other allergy-friendly ingredients. She is the reason I started this project.

In August 2008, Jo Fahringer helped me clarify my goals, and I realized I had to start my cookbook over again.

In September 2008, when I was in Seattle starting over in the making of this book, Hugh and Bettie Leiper gave me 100 percent use of their kitchen for several weeks. They enthusiastically ate all the foods I prepared and let me use their beautiful dishes, tablecloths, and decorations for my photos. Angela McClurg, who has small children, gave me recipe ideas that were busy-mom and kid friendly.

The following month, when I needed a kitchen to use in Hood River, Oregon, Kristina Burck offered hers and encouraged me to finish this cookbook. She also let me use her great dishes for my photos. From September 2008–June 2009, the following friends let me use their kitchens or dishes for cooking and photos: Paula Maden, Marily Saur, Julia Krentz, Susie Ellis, Bonita Dewberry, and Maureen Bensch. Deana Brown and Leigha Andrews gave me friendship and support whenever I baked my cookies at their church for their youth group!

My sister, Nancy Isern, who has a master's in nutrition and is now a scientist, explained why certain ingredients act the way they do and told me how to get the best results. She also supported and encouraged me with this entire project. I wrote and prepared some of these recipes in her kitchen and took some pictures using her dishes and decorations. Eric Isern, my brother-in-law, was one of my taste-testers and became a fan of allergy-friendly foods, even though he has no food allergies.

Most importantly, I need to give credit to my parents, John and Vivian Gauen, and my two grandmothers, Hattie Chesarek and Esther Gauen, who taught me to appreciate good homemade food.

I also want to thank all of the people in Youth With A Mission (YWAM) with whom I've had the privilege of cooking in YWAM kitchens around the world! They taught me different ways to prepare foods from many nations, adding to my cooking knowledge.

And finally I want to say a huge thank you to all the gracious and hard-working people at Strang Communications. With this being my first book, their enthusiasm, patience, and encouragement made the whole publishing experience stress-free, simple, and a joy.

INTRODUCTION

A NOTE ABOUT GLUTEN

The baking recipes in this book (bread, muffins, cakes, cookies, etc.) are gluten-free. However, most recipes in the chapters outside the baking section may be prepared with or without gluten, with or without dairy products, and with or without eggs. Since you, the cook, are given your choice of what specific ingredients to use in each recipe, it's up to you to carefully read the labels on the products you purchase for the recipes in this book. Be sure they are free of anything (soy, corn, food dyes, etc.) that may cause your allergic reactions.

ABOUT ALLERGY-FRIENDLY INGREDIENTS

Before using any ingredient that is labeled "allergy-free," check with your doctor to see which ones you are allowed to eat for your specific allergies. The packages containing gluten-free flour should be labeled "gluten-free." If they are not, call the company to confirm that no gluten is present. (See the appendix for a list of suppliers of allergy-friendly ingredients.)

What do I do if I can't find some of the ingredients I need?

These ingredients are usually available in the health food section of grocery stores and at your local organic or health food store. If stores in your area do not carry something you need, talk to the store manager to see if they will order it for you. The next option is to look at the appendix in this book, "Where to Purchase Allergy-Friendly Ingredients," and call the company directly to ask if they sell their products in your area. If all else fails, the ingredients may be ordered online.

Using gluten-free oatmeal flour and other kinds of gluten-free flour when baking

In some of the baking recipes in this book, the ingredient list calls for another flour in addition to the Pancake & Baking Mix. In these instances, I have recommended that you use gluten-free oatmeal flour. It adds amazing taste, texture, fiber, protein, and moistness to baked goods. It may also help lower cholesterol. Make your own oatmeal flour by putting certified gluten-free oatmeal into a food processor, flourmill, or coffee grinder. (Those who are not gluten intolerant may use the same process with either quick-cooking or old-fashioned oats.) Oatmeal flour ground in the food processor will not be as fine, and small flecks of oatmeal will be visible in the finished product, giving baked goods a whole grain look. No matter how finely oatmeal flour is milled, the taste and texture it contributes to gluten-free baked goods will be excellent.

Nonetheless, those who are allergic to oatmeal may choose other gluten-free options. Almond meal, coconut flour, hazelnut flour, or fine-ground cornmeal are all good cup-for-cup substitutes for oatmeal flour. They are also good sources of protein and fiber. Keep two or three of them on hand and use them together or separately. However, if you have made your own baking mix from scratch using a nut flour, do not use a nut flour to replace oatmeal flour when it is called for in addition to the mix. Doing so will result in too much oil and an excess of calories in the finished product.

Also, do not use any of the following kinds of flour alone as a cup-for-cup replacement for oatmeal flour: brown rice flour, white rice flour, tapioca flour, or any flour in place of oatmeal flour. When these flours are used in the right combination, though, they produce excellent results. If you cannot use any of the other alternatives to oatmeal flour I have offered in this section, make my oatmeal flour replacement mix using this exact recipe: 2 cups brown rice flour, 2 cups sorghum flour, ¾ cup white rice flour, and 1 cup tapioca flour. (Do not make any changes or substitutions to this formula.) Use the resulting mix whenever a recipe calls for oatmeal flour.

In some instances sorghum flour may be used cup-for-cup as a replacement for oatmeal flour. If a recipe calls for a ratio of two parts of Baking Mix to one part oatmeal flour or less (e.g., 1 cup Baking Mix and ⅛ to ½ cup oatmeal flour), sorghum flour may be used. But if the proportion of oatmeal flour to Baking Mix is over 50 percent (e.g., 1 cup Baking Mix and ⅔ to 1 cup oatmeal flour), sorghum flour should not be used, since its bitter taste and gritty texture will spoil the finished product.

In addition to sorghum flour, some other kinds of flour are very healthy but have unpleasant or overpowering flavors that could ruin the flavor of your baked goods if used in large quantities. These include buckwheat flour, amaranth flour, quinoa flour, or any bean flour. Only add them in very small amounts. For example, if a recipe calls for 1 cup of oatmeal flour, measure 2 tablespoons of both sorghum flour and black bean flour in the bottom of your 1-cup measure, then fill the measuring cup to the top with a combination of cornmeal flour and coconut flour.

Each kind of gluten-free flour will lend a slightly different taste and texture to baked goods, so this gives the cook some room for creativity. Have fun experimenting with the different flours and their tastes, but make no other changes to the recipes than the ones I have given you.

Dairy-free milk, cheese, sour cream, margarine, and ice cream substitutes

When preparing recipes for this book that call for milk, I used plain hemp milk because it looks thick and rich, freezes well, has a pleasant taste, and is loaded with vitamins and omega-3 fatty acids. You may use the dairy or non-dairy milk of your preference (cow, goat, hemp, soy, rice, almond, or coconut). Keep in mind that dairy milk sometimes curdles (as in escalloped potatoes), soy milk does not freeze well and tends to be chalky, and rice milk is sweet and has a thin consistency.

Many people who have allergies to dairy products do not have allergies to goat milk products. Ask your doctor if goat milk is an option for you. Goat dairy products, such as milk, butter, cheese, and kefir, are available at many grocery stores in the dairy section.

Dairy-free cheese, sour cream, margarine, and ice cream are available in grocery stores and health food stores. When looking at dairy-free labels, watch for casein and whey, which are both dairy products. Something marked "vegan" is usually dairy-free but may contain soy. Read the list of ingredients on the label to be sure it is safe for your specific food allergies.

Eggs and egg replacements to use when baking bread, cakes, cookies, muffins, etc.

In this cookbook, each gluten-free recipe that calls for eggs gives the amount needed as a cup measurement instead of as a quantity of eggs. The liquid content must be exact in gluten-free cooking or the recipe will not turn out, so use a liquid measure to be sure the amount of eggs or egg whites is precise. Egg whites may be fresh or the kind sold in cartons in the grocery store (these usually contain yellow food color).

Replacing eggs with something else

When baking, using real eggs or egg whites gives the best results, but the egg replacement I use in this book also produces good results. In each gluten-free baking recipe that calls for eggs, I give a specific egg replacement option. The amount of baking mix and sorghum flour varies when the egg replacement is used, so watch for this when doing egg-free, gluten-free baking.

Applesauce may be used to replace eggs instead of the cornstarch and water mixture I use in my recipes. To use applesauce, omit the cornstarch, tapioca flour, or potato starch, along with the water. Replace the water with the same amount of applesauce. (If it calls for ½ cup of water, use a level ½ cup of applesauce.)

Use the amount of baking powder or salt the egg-replacement recipe calls for. (Egg-replacement recipes using the Pancake and Baking Mix call for baking powder; recipes that use the Pizza Crust & Yeast Bread mix call for salt.)

Mayonnaise

Vegan mayonnaise, which contains no animal products, is available for those who may not eat eggs or dairy products. Go to the Appendix, "Where to Purchase Allergy-Friendly Ingredients," to view a few different mayonnaise products, or search the Internet for "vegan mayonnaise." Some contain soy and some are soy-free, so read the labels carefully.

Pasta

When preparing any recipe in this cookbook that calls for pasta, any pasta may be used, including gluten-free pasta made from brown rice, quinoa, or corn flour; spelt pasta; or wheat pasta made from semolina, all-purpose, or whole-wheat flour. Gluten-free pasta comes in many shapes, such as spaghetti, elbow macaroni, spirals, shells, penne, lasagna, and fettuccini.

Nuts

When a recipe calls for nuts, replace them with a different nut or dried fruit, or leave them out. If a recipe calls for peanut butter, substitute pumpkin seed butter, sunflower seed butter, or some other nut butter. (Almond and cashew nut butters are nice separately or blended.)

Rice

When a recipe calls for rice, I use white or brown basmati or jasmine rice, but use whatever rice is your personal favorite. Brown rice needs to cook for 40–45 minutes, which is 15–20 minutes longer than white rice, and sometimes needs additional water.

Butter, Shortening, and Oil

When a recipe calls for vegetable shortening, neither oil nor margarine will work. Look in the appendix, "Where to Purchase Allergy-Friendly Ingredients," for information on who makes soy-free shortening. Lard may be used in place of vegetable shortening in any of these recipes.

Some recipes indicate that salted butter may be replaced with coconut oil. Keep in mind that coconut oil contains no salt, so I recommend adding ⅛ tsp. salt whenever coconut oil is used in place of salted butter.

Sugar and sugar substitutes

I used granulated sugar or organic sugar when creating these recipes. The only sugar substitutes that may yield favorable results are those that measure cup-for-cup the same as sugar.

Syrups

When syrup is called for in a recipe in this book, I used brown rice syrup. Brown rice syrup has a nice flavor and is a complex sugar. (It is absorbed and breaks down slower than simple sugar, preventing a rapid spike in blood sugar.) When preparing a recipe that calls for brown rice syrup, either corn syrup or agave nectar may be substituted, though you may need to add more or less to get the desired sweetness. Agave nectar is made from the agave plant and has a low glycemic index. It is a little sweeter than either brown rice or corn syrup.

How to Measure Dry Ingredients

If the ingredients are not measured accurately, the recipes will not turn out correctly. Read the directions below to learn how to measure dry ingredients.

Lightly spoon flour into a measuring cup until it is slightly overfilled. (Do not pack ingredients into the measuring cup. Brown sugar is the only ingredient that needs to be packed down into the cup.) Use a straight-edged spatula or ruler to remove the excess flour, scraping once across the whole surface of the measuring cup in one direction.

Freezing

All foods baked using the Pizza Crust and Yeast Bread Mix and the Pancake and Baking Mix may be frozen for up to three months. Put them in an airtight freezer bag, press out all the air, and seal the bag shut. To protect baked goods from being crushed in the freezer, store the sealed freezer bag inside a plastic container with a lid. To thaw these items, set them out on the counter for a few hours or overnight until the baked goods come to room temperature.

Any of the main dishes may also be frozen when they are prepared with meat only or with meat in combination with brown rice pasta (other pastas do not freeze well) or rice of any kind. Freeze meat dishes in a plastic or glass freezer container with a snugly fitting lid. If there is air in the container, only freeze the dish for a month. If there is no airspace in the container, it may be frozen for up to three months. Thaw meat dishes by placing the container in which they are stored in the refrigerator overnight or for up to twenty-four hours. Reheat the items in the oven or microwave to serve them hot.

Any white sauce prepared with hemp or rice milk also freezes well.

Potatoes and vegetables tend to get mushy when they are frozen, so I do not recommend freezing any recipe that contains those.

How to Measure Liquid Ingredients

Since the amount of liquid used in gluten-free baking must be exact, always use a liquid measure when measuring eggs and other liquids called for in recipes. Place the measuring glass on a flat tabletop and pour in the liquid until the desired measurement is reached. Never hold the liquid measure in your hand, as the liquid measure will not be level, resulting in a wrong measurement. While pouring liquid into the measuring glass on the countertop, bend over so your eye is level with the measurement markings on the side of the container. Liquids will be higher around the outside edges, and this is not where the measurement should be taken. The correct measurement occurs when the flat liquid, which is in the center of the measuring glass, reaches the level of the desired measuring mark.

Equivalent Measurements

When multiplying or dividing a recipe, it is helpful to know how many teaspoons are in a tablespoon, how many tablespoons are in a cup, how many cups are in a pint, etc.

½ Tbsp.=1 ½ tsp.	⅔ cup=10 Tbsp. plus 2 tsp.
1 Tbsp.=3 tsp.	¾ cup=12 Tbsp.
⅛ cup=2 Tbsp.	⅞ cup=¾ cup plus 2 Tbsp.
¼ cup=4 Tbsp.	1 cup=16 Tbsp.
⅓ cup=5 Tbsp. plus 1 tsp.	1 pint=2 cups
⅜ cup=¼ cup plus 2 Tbsp.	1 quart=2 pints=4 cups
½ cup=8 Tbsp.	1 gallon=4 quarts=16 cups
⅝ cup=½ cup plus 2 Tbsp.	

RECIPES FOR BASIC BAKING MIXES

These mixes are easily and cheaply made in your own kitchen. Making these mixes yourself is healthy and allows you to prepare the mix to fit your own tastes and needs. Be sure to prepare the mixes exactly as they appear in the recipe in order to ensure consistent results each time.

If you do a lot of baking, you should buy each kind of flour by the case at your local grocery store. One case of the brand I buy contains four 16- to 24-ounce bags of one particular kind of flour, and my store gives a discount for purchasing by the case. But, each company packages their flour differently, so when placing an order, ask about the ounces per bag and case size of the brand of flour your store carries, as well as about discount rates for buying in bulk.

Some of these kinds of flour are available in the bulk-bin section of the health food section of grocery stores. Refer to the appendix, "Where to Purchase Allergy-Friendly Ingredients," to find out where gluten-free flour and corn-free xanthan gum may be purchased.

Money-saving tip

Save money by using a flour mill to grind your own white rice and brown rice flour, cornmeal, etc. I don't have a flour mill, but a coffee grinder works to mill some kinds of flour.

For those who would rather have ready-made mixes made with high-quality flour, the Celebrating Food!® Pancake & Baking Mix and Celebrating Food!® Pizza Crust & Yeast Bread Mix Mix are both available online at www.celebratingfoodglutenfree.com. It is important to note that these mixes are not interchangeable; one is for use with my yeast bread recipes, and the other is used in all my other baking recipes, which use baking powder. Both mixes have outstanding flavor. The Celebrating Food!® Pancake & Baking Mix is oatmeal-free as well as gluten-free, but it does contain small amounts of corn products.

PIZZA CRUST AND YEAST BREAD MIX

Makes approximately 17 cups

This is the baking mix used for yeast dough to make bread, hamburger buns, sandwich rolls, focaccia bread, and pizza crust.

Ingredient	Measure	Weight and Special Instructions
white rice flour	4 ¼ cups	24 oz. (1 lb. 8 oz. or 680 grams)
rice bran*	2 ⅛ cups	9 oz. (or 255 grams)
salt	2 Tbsp.	1.4 oz. or 39.69 grams
xanthan gum	¼ cup	1.28 oz. or 36.28 grams
sorghum flour	4 ½ cups	22 oz. (1 lb. 6 oz. or 623.69 grams)
tapioca flour	4 ½ cups	20 oz. (1 lb. 4 oz. or 567 grams)

Directions

Place white rice flour, rice bran, salt, and xanthan gum into a large bowl, in the order given. Use a large spoon to turn mixture over and over, turning bowl and scraping across the bottom of the bowl each time. Baked goods will only turn out correctly when the salt and xanthan gum are evenly distributed throughout the mix, so good mixing is important.

Add the sorghum and tapioca flour, and mix it thoroughly again.

To ensure that the ingredients trapped in the bottom of the bowl are well mixed, tip the mixture into a different large bowl and mix thoroughly yet one more time. Now the mix is ready to be used.

PANCAKE AND BAKING MIX

Makes approximately 29 cups

Ingredient	Measure	Weight and Special Instructions
brown rice flour	8 ½ cups	48 oz. (3 lbs. or 1360.77 grams)
potato starch	1 cup	6.85 oz. (or 194.19 grams)
baking powder	¾ cup plus 2 Tbsp.	6.75 oz. (or 191.36 grams) Gently turn the can of baking powder upside down three times before measuring to "fluff" up the baking powder. To save time, purchase a large baking powder container that your ¼-cup measure will fit into.
salt	3 Tbsp.	2.1 oz. (or 59.53 grams)

*Rice bran adds fiber and nutrition. It also helps the bread to turn a nice golden brown. Those who do not need the extra fiber from rice bran can use brown rice flour.

RASPBERRY ICED TEA

Makes 8 cups (½ gallon or 2 quarts)

This is just as refreshing as the powder concentrate that is purchased at the grocery store, but this one is free of food dye and made with healthy green tea, and you can decide how to sweeten it.

2 quarts filtered water
2 raspberry herbal tea bags
2 green tea bags (or plain black tea)
½ cup granulated sugar, honey, or sweetener of choice

Bring 2 cups water to a boil in small saucepan. Remove from heat and add tea bags. Let it steep for 10 minutes. Remove the bags, pressing out all liquid. Pour the resulting tea concentrate into a half-gallon container and, while it is still warm, stir in sugar. Fill the container to the top with filtered water. Chill the tea in the refrigerator several hours or overnight.

Note

Read herbal tea bag labels to be sure that no artificial colors are present. Only purchase tea that has all-natural ingredients.

To fill a one-gallon jar, double the recipe.

Variation

- **Mint iced tea:** Replace the raspberry tea bags with mint tea bags.
- **Peach iced tea:** Replace the raspberry tea bags with peach tea bags.

PART TWO

BREADS

APPLE CINNAMON BREAD

Makes one large loaf

1 tsp. apple cider vinegar
2 ½ cups applesauce
½ cup eggs (2–3 eggs) or egg whites*
¼ cup canola oil or other oil of choice
½ cup brown sugar
3 cups Pizza Crust and Yeast Bread Mix
1 cup gluten-free oatmeal flour or other substitute from p. 2
2 Tbsp. cinnamon
1 package (2 ½ tsp.) active dry yeast

---

* To replace eggs, measure 2 Tbsp. cornstarch, tapioca flour, or potato starch into a liquid measure. Add ¼ tsp. salt. Fill liquid measure to the ½-cup mark with water and mix the contents of the measuring cup together. Add the mixture in place of eggs. Increase the Yeast Bread Mix to 3 ⅛ cups and decrease the flour to ⅞ cup.

Bread machine method

Measure all ingredients into your bread machine in the order given. Set the bread machine on "normal/white" and start it.

After the mixing starts, if any dry ingredients are stuck to the side of the pan, use a rubber spatula to push them down into the dough.

When the bread cycle is finished, remove the bake pan and invert the pan on a cooling rack. Gently shake the loaf out of the pan and remove the paddle from the bottom of the bread.

Mixer and oven method

Grease a 9- x 5-inch loaf pan. Set aside. Heat the oven to 120°.

Measure all the ingredients into the mixing bowl of a stand mixer fitted with the paddle attachment. Blend on low until all the ingredients are moistened. Mix the dough on medium speed for 1 minute or until all the ingredients are blended and the dough is smooth. Scrape down the sides and bottom of the bowl with a rubber spatula and mix the dough again.

Cover the bowl with a towel, turn the oven off, and place the bowl into the warm oven. Let the dough rise until it has doubled, about 30 minutes. Carefully transfer the risen dough to the prepared bread pan, being careful not to press out the air, and level it with a rubber spatula.

Heat the oven to 350°. (The dough will continue to rise in the pan while the oven is preheating.) Once the oven reaches the baking temperature, place the loaf in the hot oven and bake it for 40 to 45 minutes. Remove the bread from the oven, turn the pan on its side, and gently shake the loaf out of its baking pan. The bread cuts best with sharp knife after it is completely cool.

Store the bread in an airtight bag with a paper towel in it. The paper towel will keep the bread from sweating.

BAKING POWDER BISCUITS

Makes 12 biscuits

2 ¼ cups Pancake and Baking Mix
1 ⅝ cups gluten-free oatmeal flour or other substitute from p. 2
4 tsp. baking powder
2 packages active dry yeast (5 tsp.)
¾ cup vegetable shortening or lard
2 cups cold water
3 Tbsp. salted dairy-free margarine or butter, melted (to brush tops of biscuits)

Preheat the oven to 400°. Grease a baking sheet.

In a medium-sized mixing bowl, measure the Pancake and Baking Mix, flour, baking powder, and yeast. Mix ingredients with a fork. Cut in shortening using a pastry blender until the shortening is totally incorporated into the dry ingredients. Add the water and mix with a fork just until all the ingredients are blended.

Divide the dough into twelve equal parts and shape each one into a circle about 1 ¼ inches high and 2 ¾ inches wide. Place the biscuits on a prepared baking sheet about ½ inch apart. Dribble a few drops of melted margarine over the top of each biscuit.

Put the biscuits in the oven and bake for 15–18 minutes until they are golden brown and centers are done. Serve hot or cold.

BANANA BREAD

Makes one 9- x 5-inch loaf

This bread is moist and loaded with banana flavor!

½ cup canola oil or other oil of choice
1 cup brown sugar
½ cup eggs (2–3 eggs) or egg whites*
2 tsp. vanilla extract
1 ½ cups mashed overripe bananas (3–4 bananas)
2 ⅓ cups Pancake and Baking Mix
¾ cup chopped walnuts or nuts of choice (optional; these may also be replaced with allergy-free or semi-sweet chocolate chips)

Coat one 9- x 5- x 3-inch bread pan with nonstick cooking spray (do not use a smaller pan, as bread will have difficulty getting done in the center). Preheat the oven to 350°.

Transfer the oil, brown sugar, eggs, vanilla, and mashed bananas to the mixing bowl of a stand mixer fitted with the paddle attachment. Beat on low and then on medium-low speed until all the ingredients are blended.

---

* To replace the eggs, measure 2 Tbsp. cornstarch, tapioca flour, or potato starch into a liquid measure. Add a scant ½ tsp. baking powder. Fill the container to the ½-cup mark with water and mix the ingredients together. Add the mixture in place of the eggs. Add an additional ⅛ cup Baking Mix.

Turn off the mixer and add the Pancake and Baking Mix. Blend ingredients on the lowest speed until all dry ingredients are moistened. Stop the mixer to scrape down the sides and then blend on medium speed for another minute. Stir in the walnuts.

Pour the batter into a prepared pan and level with a spatula. Bake for 63–68 minutes or until a toothpick inserted in the center comes out clean and the loaf feels firm when the top is lightly pressed. If the nuts are added, the bread will need to bake for 65–68 minutes.

Place the loaf on a cooling rack for 10 minutes. Then turn the loaf pan on its side to allow the bread to gently slide out. Turn the loaf right side up and leave it on cooling rack until it reaches room temperature. Store the bread in an airtight container.

CARAMEL ROLLS

Makes 12 giant-muffin-sized rolls

These may be prepared dairy-free.

Rolls
one recipe Gluten-Free Sandwich Rolls

Caramel Filling
1 ½ cups brown sugar
¾ cup salted butter, dairy-free margarine, or coconut oil

Make one batch of Gluten-Free Sandwich Rolls according to the recipe on page 27 and divide the dough in half.

Mix caramel filling ingredients in a small bowl and divide the filling in half.

Preheat the oven to 400°. Grease twelve giant muffin tins.

Sprinkle half of the caramel filling evenly between the twelve muffin cups. Divide half of the sandwich roll dough equally between the muffin cups, placing the dough over the caramel filling in each one. Repeat those two layers again.

Place the muffin pan on a cookie sheet to protect your oven in case some of the caramel boils over during baking and put them in the oven. After the rolls have baked for 20 minutes, check to see if they are done. The rolls will be golden brown on top and the caramel will be very bubbly.

When they are done baking, remove the caramel rolls from the oven. Lay a clean cookie sheet over the top of the muffin pan and flip the muffins upside down onto the clean cookie sheet. Do this immediately after the rolls come out of the oven, before the caramel hardens and makes the muffins stick in the pan. Lift the muffin pan off the caramel rolls. When the pan has cooled completely, pour some warm water in it to soak off any caramel that remains in the pan. (Never put water into a hot baking pan. If the pan is metal, the cold water may warp the pan. If the pan is glass, it will shatter.)

Let the rolls cool at least 15 minutes before serving. (Otherwise, people may burn their mouths on the hot caramel filling.)

I serve the rolls upside down so the caramel is visible, but once the rolls are cool, they may be turned right side up and frosted with Buttercream Frosting (see p. 59).

CORNBREAD WITH HONEY BUTTER

Makes one 9-inch square or 7- x 11-inch pan

⅞ cup cornmeal
1 ¼ cups Pancake and Baking Mix
⅛ tsp. salt
½ cup granulated sugar
½ cup canola oil or other oil of choice
½ cup eggs (2–3 eggs) or egg whites*
1 ¼ cups dairy or non-dairy milk
Serve with Honey Butter (see p. 130)

Preheat the oven to 350°. Grease a 9-inch square or 7- x 11-inch baking pan. Set aside.

Transfer the cornmeal, Pancake and Baking Mix, salt, and sugar to the mixing bowl of a stand mixer fitted with the paddle attachment. Mix the ingredients on low to combine. Add the oil, eggs, and milk. Mix on medium speed until well blended, scrape down the sides and bottom of the mixing bowl, and blend again until all the ingredients are combined. Pour the batter into a prepared pan, scraping out the mixing bowl with a rubber scraper.

Bake for 35–37 minutes or until a toothpick inserted in the center comes out clean and the top feels firm when lightly pressed.

---

* To replace the eggs, measure 2 Tbsp. cornstarch, tapioca flour, or potato starch into a liquid measure. Add ½ tsp. baking powder. Fill the container to the ½-cup mark with water and mix the ingredients together. Add the mixture in place of eggs. Increase the amount of baking mix to 1 ½ cups, and decrease the flour to ⅝ cup (½ cup plus 2 Tbsp.).

Note

Those who are allergic to cornmeal may substitute oatmeal flour or the substitutes on p. 2 in place of cornmeal. Add ¼–½ tsp. turmeric for a nice yellow color.

CRANBERRY BREAD

Makes one 8 ½- x 4 ½-inch loaf

Fresh cranberries and orange remind us of Thanksgiving and Christmas.

2 cups Pancake and Baking Mix
1 cup granulated sugar
⅓ cup grated orange rind (the rind of 1 orange)
juice from 1 orange plus water to make ¾ cup
¼ cup eggs (1–2 eggs) or egg whites*
2 Tbsp. canola oil or other oil of choice
2 cups fresh cranberries, cut in half
½ cup walnuts or dried fruit of choice

Preheat the oven to 350°. Grease an 8 ½- x 4 ½-inch loaf pan. Set aside.

Fit a stand mixer with the paddle attachment. Measure Pancake and Baking Mix and sugar into the mixing bowl of stand mixer. Mix on low until the ingredients are thoroughly blended. Add the orange rind, juice and water, egg, and canola oil. Mix on medium-low speed until well blended. Turn off the mixer, scrape down the sides and bottom of the bowl, and mix again. Add the cranberries and nuts, mixing just until blended.

Pour the batter into the prepared pan and level with rubber spatula. Bake 60–65 minutes or until a toothpick inserted in the center comes out clean and the loaf feels firm when the top is lightly pressed.

Place the pan on a wire rack to cool for 10 minutes. Gently shake the bread out of the pan, and it leave on the cooling rack until the loaf reaches room temperature. Store the bread in an airtight container.

---

* To replace the eggs, measure 1 Tbsp. cornstarch, tapioca flour, or potato starch into a liquid measure. Add a scant ¼ tsp. baking powder. Fill the container to the ¼-cup mark with water and mix the ingredients together. Add the mixture in place of eggs. Increase the amount of baking mix to 2 ⅛ cups.

FIVE-STAR SANDWICH BREAD

Makes one loaf

The taste and texture of this bread
is very pleasant. Make it in the
bread machine to save time.
This may be prepared dairy-free
and egg-free.

1 tsp. apple cider vinegar
1 ½ cups warm water (or milk of
    choice), 115°
¾ cup eggs (3–4 eggs) or egg
    whites*

¼ cup olive oil or other oil of choice
¼ cup granulated sugar
2 ⅞ cups Pizza Crust and Yeast Bread Mix
1 cup gluten-free oatmeal flour or other substitute from p. 2
1 package (2 ½ tsp.) active dry yeast

Bread machine method

Measure all ingredients into a bread machine in the order given. Set the
bread machine to "normal/white." Start the machine. After the mixing starts,
if any dry ingredients are stuck to the side of the pan, use a rubber spatula to
push them down into the dough. When the bread cycle is finished, remove the
baking pan and invert it onto a cooling rack. Gently shake the loaf out of the
pan and remove the paddle from the bottom of the bread.

Mixer and oven method

Grease a 9- x 5-inch loaf pan. Set aside. Heat the oven to 120°.
Measure all the ingredients into the mixing bowl of a stand mixer fitted with
the paddle attachment. Blend on low until all the ingredients are moistened.
Mix the dough on medium speed for 1 minute or until all the ingredients are
blended and the dough is smooth. Scrape down the sides and bottom of the
bowl with a rubber spatula and mix the dough again. Cover the bowl with a
towel, turn the oven off, and place the bowl into the warm oven. Let the dough
rise until it has doubled, about 30 minutes. Carefully transfer the risen dough

* To replace the eggs, measure 3 Tbsp. cornstarch, tapioca flour, or potato starch into a
liquid measure. Add ¼ tsp. salt. Fill the container to the ¾-cup mark with water, and mix
the ingredients together. Add the mixture in place of eggs. Increase the amount of yeast
bread mix to 3 cups and decrease the flour to ⅞ cup.

to a bread pan, being careful not to press out the air, and level it with a rubber spatula.

Heat the oven to 350°. (The bread will continue to rise in the pan while the oven is preheating.) Once the oven reaches the baking temperature, place the bread in the hot oven and bake for 38–40 minutes. Remove the loaf from the oven and cool it in the pan for 10 minutes. Then turn the pan on its side and gently shake the loaf out of the pan.

The bread cuts best with a sharp knife after it is completely cool.

Variation

- **Five-Star Sandwich and Seeds Bread:** Prepare Five-Star Sandwich Bread, but before mixing the dough, add 3 Tbsp. of any combination of the following: sunflower seeds, whole grain teff, flax seeds, poppy seeds, millet seeds, or amaranth grain. Just before baking the bread, sprinkle the top with 1 Tbsp. sesame seeds (or other seeds of choice).

PUMPKIN QUICK BREAD

Makes one 9- x 5-inch loaf

The scent of pumpkin and spices reminds me of fall. It is good with or without nuts.

2 ⅓ cups Pancake and Baking Mix
1 ½ cups granulated sugar
1 tsp. cinnamon
1 tsp. nutmeg
1 tsp. cloves
15 ounces (1 ¾ cups) canned or
    freshly cooked and cooled pumpkin
½ cup eggs (2–3 eggs) or egg whites*
¼ cup canola oil or other oil of choice
¾ cup chopped walnuts or raisins (optional; any fruit or dried nut may be used)

Preheat the oven to 350°. Grease a 9- x 5-inch loaf pan. Set aside.
Measure the Pancake and Baking Mix, sugar, and all the spices into the

---

* To replace the eggs, measure 2 Tbsp. cornstarch, tapioca flour, or potato starch into a liquid measure. Add a scant ½ tsp. baking powder. Fill the container to the ½-cup mark with water and mix the ingredients together. Add the mixture in place of the eggs. Add an additional ⅛ cup Baking Mix.

mixing bowl of stand mixer fitted with the paddle attachment. Mix on low until the ingredients are thoroughly blended. Add the pumpkin, egg, and canola oil. Mix on medium-low speed until well blended. Turn off the mixer, scrape down the sides and bottom of the bowl, and mix again. Add nuts and mix just until blended.

Pour the batter into the prepared pan and level with a rubber spatula. Bake for 62–65 minutes or until a toothpick inserted in the center comes out clean and the loaf feels firm when the top is lightly pressed. If nuts or raisins are added, the bread will need to bake for 65–68 minutes.

Place the loaf on a wire rack to cool for 10 minutes. Gently shake the bread out of the pan, and leave the loaf right side up on the cooling rack until it reaches room temperature. Store the bread in an airtight container.

SANDWICH ROLLS/ HAMBURGER BUNS

Makes 12 rolls for 12 sandwiches

3 cups warm water
2 packages yeast (5 tsp.)
2 Tbsp. granulated sugar
½ cup canola oil or other oil of choice
3 cups Pizza Crust and Yeast Bread Mix
1 cup gluten-free oatmeal flour or other substitute from p. 2
3 Tbsp. melted salted butter, dairy-free margarine, or coconut oil
1 Tbsp. poppy seeds or sesame seeds (optional)

In a small bowl, combine the warm water, yeast, sugar, and oil. Add the Pizza Crust and Yeast Bread Mix and flour. Mix with a wooden spoon until all the ingredients are blended.

For two 9- x 13-inch pans

Preheat the oven to 400°.

Grease two 9- x 13-inch baking pans. Divide the dough equally between the two pans and smooth the tops with a spatula. Brush with melted butter and sprinkle with poppy seeds. Bake the rolls for 20–25 minutes.

Cool the bread in the pans until they reach room temperature. Cut each pan into twelve equally sized squares. Use one square for the bottom of the sandwich and use another square for the top. This makes twelve full sandwiches.

For a king-sized muffin pan

Grease twelve king-sized muffin cup slots. Divide the dough equally between the cups. Brush the tops with melted butter and sprinkle with poppy seeds.

Cover the rolls with a towel and set in a warm place to rise for 20–30 minutes.

Preheat the oven to 400°. Place the rolls in the oven and bake them for 20–25 minutes or until they are lightly browned and the bread is done. Remove the rolls from the oven and place them on cooling racks.

Cool the rolls in the pan for 10 minutes, then invert the pans onto a cooling rack and finish cooling the rolls until they are room temperature. To make a sandwich, cut the rolls in half.

Variations

- **Onion rolls:** Add 2 Tbsp. dried onion flakes.
- **Healthy seed rolls:** Add 1 tsp. each: flax seeds, poppy seeds, and sunflower seeds (or seeds of choice).
- **Herb rolls:** Add 1 Tbsp. dried parsley and 1 ½ Tbsp. Italian seasoning.
- **Stuffing-flavored rolls:** Add 1 Tbsp. rubbed sage, ½ tsp. celery seed, and 2 tsp. dried onion flakes.

FOCACCIA BREAD (OR PIZZA CRUST)

Makes one 12- x 16-inch jellyroll pan or one round pizza pan

This tender but chewy bread is also great for sandwiches.

Crust

2 cups warm water, 115°
1 package (2 ½ tsp.) active dry yeast
3 Tbsp. olive oil or other oil of
    choice
1 3/4 cups Pizza Crust and Yeast Bread Mix
1 cup gluten-free oatmeal flour or other substitute from p. 2
3/4 cup brown rice flour
1/2 cup tapioca flour
1 Tbsp. Italian seasoning

Topping

⅓ cup salted butter, non-dairy margarine, or coconut oil, melted
½ tsp. dried rosemary
½ tsp. dried thyme
½ tsp. garlic powder

Put all crust ingredients into a bread machine in the order given. Set the bread machine to the "pasta/dough" setting, so that it mixes and allows the dough to rise but not to bake. (If mixing by hand or in a stand mixer, measure all the ingredients into a mixing bowl and mix until they are all well blended. Sit the bowl in a warm place [about 120° F] to rise for about 1 hour or until the dough has doubled.)

Coat a jellyroll pan or round pizza pan with cooking spray or other shortening of your choice. Tip the focaccia dough onto the pan. Coat your hands with some oil and gently press the dough to fill the pan completely.

Spread melted butter, margarine, or coconut oil over the surface of the dough and sprinkle with topping spices.

Let the dough rise while the oven preheats to 425°. When the oven reaches the desired temperature, bake the bread for 20–22 minutes. If the focaccia needs to brown more, put it under the broiler. (Remove the focaccia from the oven and turn on the broiler, leaving the oven door ajar. When the broiler is hot, place the bread on the rack closest to the broiler and bake for another 3–5 minutes, turning the pan around frequently, until dough is golden brown. Remove the pan from the oven. Cut the focaccia into desired sizes with a pizza cutter while it is still hot.

For a great snack, serve focaccia strips with pizza sauce.

Variation

- **Mexican focaccia:** When making the dough, substitute 1 Tbsp. chili powder for the Italian seasoning. Omit the rosemary and thyme from the topping and replace them with 1 tsp. cumin and ½ tsp. Mexican oregano (or regular oregano).

If using gluten-free or old-fashioned oatmeal, pulse it in a food processor until it is the size of quick-cooking oatmeal. Set aside.

In a very small bowl, mix the brown sugar, vanilla, cinnamon, and salt. Transfer the oatmeal to a large bowl and add the brown sugar mixture to it. Distribute the brown sugar evenly throughout mixture by rubbing it between your fingers. Add raisins and nuts, and use your fingers to separate any raisins that stick together. Stir the mixture to distribute raisins and nuts throughout the oatmeal mixture.

Store in large, airtight container with a ½-cup scoop inside for easy measuring. A gallon-sized jar is a practical place to store your oatmeal mix.

To serve the oatmeal, measure ½ cup of the oatmeal mix, plus ½ cup of either water or dairy or non-dairy milk in a cereal bowl. Microwave for 1 minute, and then check for doneness. Cook the oatmeal until it reaches the desired consistency. Adjust the amount of liquid to get your "dream bowl of oatmeal." (This may also be prepared on the stove top.)

Variations
- **Maple instant oatmeal:** Add 1 Tbsp. maple extract.

PANCAKES

Makes 8-10 medium pancakes

1 ½ cups Pancake and Baking Mix
½ cup gluten-free oatmeal flour or
    substitute from p. 2
¼ cup granulated sugar
2 Tbsp. canola oil or other oil of
    choice
1 tsp. vanilla extract
enough dairy or non-dairy milk to
    make 2 cups total when added to
    the oil and vanilla

Heat a pancake griddle to 350° or heat a nonstick frying pan on the stove over medium-low heat. Whisk the dry ingredients together in a small mixing bowl. Measure the oil and vanilla into a 2-cup liquid measure. Add enough milk to make 2 cups. Whisk the wet and dry ingredients together.

Grease the griddle or frying pan. Pour about ⅓ cup of batter per pancake, leaving at least 1 inch between pancakes. Immediately smooth the batter with a rubber spatula until the pancake is ¼–⅜ inch thick. Cook 2 to 2 ½ minutes per side, until golden brown.

Variations

- **Cornmeal or buckwheat pancakes:** Replace ½ cup oatmeal flour with 1/2 cup cornmeal or buckwheat flour.
- **Apple pancakes:** Add 1 apple, peeled and cut into thin slices, 2 tsp. cinnamon, and an additional 2 Tbsp. granulated sugar.
- **Banana pancakes:** Increase the amount of Baking Mix to 1 3/4 cups; omit the oatmeal flour; and reduce the amount of milk in the oil, vanilla, and milk mixture so it totals 1 ½ cups. Add 2 mashed bananas (1 cup).
- **Pumpkin or sweet potato pancakes:** Increase the amount of Baking Mix to 1 3/4 cups; omit the oatmeal flour; and reduce the amount of milk in the oil, vanilla, and milk mixture so it totals 1 ½ cups. Add 1 cup puréed pumpkin or sweet potato and 2 tsp. nutmeg or pumpkin pie spice. You may also add an additional 2 Tbsp. granulated sugar (according to taste).
- **Gingerbread pancakes:** Reduce the amount of milk in the oil, vanilla, and milk mixture so it totals 1 ⅔ cup. Add ⅓ cup molasses, 2 Tbsp. ginger, 1 Tbsp. cinnamon, and 1 ½ tsp. nutmeg.
- **Blueberry pancakes (or any other berry):** Add 1 cup fresh or dried blueberries, cherries, strawberries, blackberries, raisins, chopped dates, etc.
- **Chocolate chip or nut pancakes:** Add 1 cup allergy-free chocolate chips or chopped nuts (any kind) to any recipe on this page.

BLUEBERRY STREUSEL COFFEECAKE

Makes one 9-inch round pan or 12 muffins

Streusel
½ cup chopped pecans (or nuts of choice)
2 tsp. cinnamon
¼ cup gluten-free oatmeal flour or other substitute from p. 2
1 Tbsp. brown sugar
1 ½ Tbsp. salted butter or dairy-free margarine

Coffeecake

1 ½ cups frozen blueberries
⅓ cup canola oil or other oil of choice
¾ cup granulated sugar
⅜ cup eggs (about 2 eggs) or egg whites*
1 tsp. vanilla extract
1 cup Pancake and Baking Mix
¾ cup gluten-free oatmeal flour or other substitute from p. 2, divided
⅝ cup dairy or dairy-free milk

Preheat the oven to 350°. Spray a 9-inch square baking pan with nonstick cooking spray or put cupcake papers in muffin pan. (If you wish to double the recipe, you may bake the cake in a 9- x 13-inch pan.)

Measure all streusel topping ingredients into a small bowl. Rub butter into the dry ingredients using your fingers. Set aside.

Measure the blueberries and ¼ cup flour into a small bowl. Toss to coat. Set aside.

Add the oil, sugar, eggs, and vanilla to the mixing bowl of a stand mixer fitted with the paddle attachment. Mix on low speed until blended.

Turn off the mixer and add the Pancake and Baking Mix and ½ cup flour. Blend on the lowest speed until all the dry ingredients are moistened. Add the milk and mix on low until well blended. Stop the mixer to scrape down the sides, and then blend on medium speed for another minute.

Add the blueberries and the rest of the flour. Stir the batter just enough to distribute the berries evenly and incorporate the flour.

Pour the batter into a prepared 9-inch round pan or twelve muffin tins and level the batter with a spatula. Sprinkle the streusel evenly over the cake.

Bake at 350° until a toothpick inserted in the center comes out clean and the top of the cake feels firm when it is lightly pressed. For 8- or 9-inch layers, bake for 45–48 minutes. Muffins will bake for 27–32 minutes. Serve the coffeecake warm or cold.

* To replace eggs, measure 1 ½ Tbsp. cornstarch, tapioca flour, or potato starch into a liquid measure. Add ¼ tsp. baking powder. Fill the container to the ⅜-cup mark with water and mix the ingredients together. Add the mixture in place of eggs. Increase the amount of Baking Mix to 1 ¼ cups and decrease flour to ½ cup.

BANANA MUFFINS

Makes 12 king-sized muffins

1 ½ cups granulated sugar
½ cup canola oil or other oil of choice
½ cup eggs (2–3 eggs) or egg whites*
1 cup dairy or non-dairy milk
1 ½ Tbsp. vanilla extract
2 ¼ cups mashed overripe bananas (4–5 bananas)
1 ¾ cups Pancake and Baking Mix
1 ¼ cups gluten-free oatmeal flour or other substitute from p. 2
1 ½ cups chopped walnuts (optional)

Preheat the oven to 350°. Grease twelve king-sized muffin tin cups. Set aside.

Measure the sugar, oil, eggs, milk, and vanilla into the mixing bowl of a stand mixer fitted with the paddle attachment. Mix on medium-low until well blended. Add the mashed bananas and blend again on medium-low speed.

Add the Pancake and Baking Mix and flour. Mix on low until the flour is moistened, then turn speed to medium and mix until well blended. Turn off the mixer and scrape down the sides and bottom of bowl, then mix again until the batter is smooth.

Use a small ladle to scoop the dough equally into each of the twelve muffin cups, filling them about three-quarters full. Shake the pan gently to level the batter. Sprinkle walnuts over the top. Place the pan in the oven and bake for 30–35 minutes. The muffins are done when a toothpick inserted in the center of one muffin comes out clean and the top of the muffin springs back when gently pressed.

Remove the muffins from oven and place the pan on a cooling rack for 10 minutes. Tip the pan and gently shake the muffins out of the tin. Place them right side up on a cooling rack until they reach room temperature.

_____

* To replace eggs, measure 2 Tbsp. cornstarch, tapioca flour, or potato starch into a liquid measure. Add ½ tsp. baking powder. Fill the container to the ½-cup mark with water and mix the ingredients together. Add the mixture in place of eggs. Increase the amount of Baking Mix to 2 cups and decrease flour to 1 cup.

minutes. Tip the muffin pan and gently shake the muffins out of the tin. Place the muffins right side up on a cooling rack until they cool down to room temperature.

Note

The recipe above produces a fudgy, decadent muffin with a flat top. For a lighter, dome-shaped muffin, use the recipe above but decrease the eggs to ½ cup and decrease the flour to ¾ cup.

CINNAMON SPICE COFFEECAKE

Makes a 9-inch square pan

Cake
¼ cup vegetable shortening or lard
¾ cup granulated sugar
¼ cup eggs (1–2 eggs) or egg whites*
1 tsp. vanilla extract
⅞ cup Pancake and Baking Mix
⅔ cup gluten-free oatmeal flour or
　　 other substitute from p. 2
½ tsp. nutmeg
½ tsp. allspice
¾ cup dairy or dairy-free milk

Topping
¼ cup granulated sugar
2 tsp. cinnamon

Preheat the oven to 350°. Spray a 9-inch square baking pan with nonstick cooking spray.

Combine the shortening, sugar, eggs, and vanilla in the mixing bowl of a stand mixer fitted with a paddle attachment. Beat the ingredients on medium to medium-high speed until blended.

Turn off the mixer and add the Pancake and Baking Mix, flour, nutmeg, allspice, and milk. Blend the mixture on the lowest speed until all the dry ingredients are moistened. Stop the mixer to scrape down the sides, and then continue to blend on medium speed for another minute.

Pour the batter into the prepared pan and level it with a spatula.

---

* To replace the eggs, measure 1 Tbsp. cornstarch, tapioca flour, or potato starch into a liquid measure. Add a scant ¼ tsp. baking powder. Fill the container to the ½-cup mark with water and mix the ingredients together. Add the mixture in place of eggs. Increase the amount of Baking Mix to 1 cup and decrease the flour to ½ cup plus ½ Tbsp.

Mix the topping ingredients and shake them evenly over the cake.

Bake the coffeecake for 28–31 minutes or until a toothpick inserted in the center comes out clean and the top of the cake feels firm when it is lightly pressed. Serve warm or cold.

POTATO PANCAKES

Makes 4 pancakes

1 pound potatoes (or 1 ¼ cups left-over mashed potatoes)
2 Tbsp. finely minced onion
2 Tbsp. Pancake and Baking Mix
⅛–¼ tsp. garlic salt (or regular salt)
⅛ tsp. black pepper
1–2 Tbsp. chopped fresh cilantro
½ cup dairy or non-dairy milk
2 Tbsp. canola oil or other oil of choice

Wash the potatoes and place them in a one-quart casserole dish with 1 Tbsp. water. Cover with a snuggly fitting lid. Put the dish in the microwave and cook on high for 10 minutes. When 10 minutes is over, let the potatoes sit in the casserole dish without removing the lid for 2 minutes.

Remove the lid and pull the skin off the potatoes. (You may also leave the skin on the potatoes.) Place the skinned potatoes back into the casserole dish and mash them with a potato masher or with the back of a fork. Add all the remaining ingredients except the oil and whip the mixture with a fork until they are light and fluffy. (If using leftover mashed potatoes, omit the salt, pepper, and milk.)

Place a large nonstick frying pan on the stove and add 2 Tbsp. oil. Turn the heat to medium so the pan can heat up while the pancakes are being shaped. Divide the potato mixture into four equal parts. Flatten out each part. You should have four pancakes about 4 inches across and ⅜ inch thick.

Place the potato pancakes side-by-side into the hot oil in the pan. Cook the pancakes until they are golden brown, about 6 minutes per side.

Note

When the oil is heating while the potato pancakes are being shaped, work quickly. If the oil starts smoking, it is too hot. Oil that has reached its smoke point should never be used, as it contains cancer-causing carcinogens.

Cool the layers in the pans for 10 minutes before inverting them onto a serving plate. (The 9- x 13-inch cake does not need to be removed from the pan). Cool the cake completely before frosting.

Variations
- **Coconut cake:** Stir in 1 cup sweetened flaked coconut.
- **Spice cake:** Omit the almond extract. Add 2 Tbsp. cinnamon, 1 Tbsp. nutmeg, 1 Tbsp. ginger, and ½ Tbsp. cloves.

CHOCOLATE STAMPEDE CAKE

Makes one 9- x 13—inch cake or

two 8- or 9-inch layers

This cake has full-volume fudge flavor. A stampede may occur at serving time!

1 cup canola oil or other oil of choice
2 ¾ cups brown sugar
2 tsp. vanilla extract
¾ cup eggs (3–4 eggs) or egg whites*
2 cups Pancake and Baking Mix
1 ⅜ cups gluten-free oatmeal flour or other substitute from p. 2
¾ cup baking cocoa
2 cups water
one recipe Chocolate or Chocolate Peppermint Frosting (see p. 59)

Preheat the oven to 350°. Grease a 9- x 13-inch pan or two 8- or 9-inch cake pans. Set aside.

In a stand mixer fitted with the paddle attachment, measure the oil, brown sugar, vanilla, and eggs. Mix on low until the ingredients are well blended.

In a separate bowl, stir together the Pancake and Baking Mix, flour, and cocoa. Then add the flour mixture to the mixing bowl, along with the water. Mix on low for about 30 seconds. Turn the speed to medium and mix for another 30 seconds. Stop the mixer and scrape down the sides and bottom of the bowl with a rubber spatula and then mix again until all the ingredients are well blended.

---

* To replace the eggs, measure 3 Tbsp. cornstarch, tapioca flour, or potato starch into a liquid measure. Add a scant ¾ tsp. baking powder. Fill the container to the ¾-cup mark with water and mix the ingredients together. Add the mixture in place of eggs. Increase the amount of Baking Mix to 2 ⅜ cups and decrease the flour to 1 cup.

Pour the batter into the prepared pan(s) and level with a rubber spatula. For a 9- x 13-inch cake, bake for 44–49 minutes. For two 8 or 9-inch layers, bake 35–40 minutes or until a toothpick inserted in the center of the cake comes out clean and the top of the cake feels firm when lightly pressed.

Cool the layers in the baking pans for 10 minutes. (The 9- x 13-inch cake should be left in the pan to cool.) Cool the cake completely before frosting.

Variations

- **Chocolate mint cake:** Add 1 tsp. mint (or peppermint) extract when the vanilla is added.
- **Chocolate mocha cake:** Replace 1 cup of water with 1 cup cooled brewed coffee. Extreme coffee lovers should replace 2 cups of water with 2 cups cooled brewed coffee.

CARROT CAKE

Makes one 9- x 13-inch cake or two 8- or 9-inch layers

Carrot cake has always been a favorite of mine. This gluten-free version will not disappoint you or your guests!

½ cup canola oil or other oil of choice
1 ¾ cups brown sugar
¾ cup eggs (3–4 eggs) or egg whites*

16 oz. crushed pineapple, juice and all
2 cups Pancake and Baking Mix
1 cup gluten-free oatmeal flour or other substitute from p. 2
2 Tbsp. cinnamon
3 cups grated carrots
1 cup chopped walnuts or raisins
one recipe Buttercream Frosting (see p. 59)

_____

* To replace the eggs, measure 3 Tbsp. cornstarch, tapioca flour, or potato starch into a liquid measure. Add a scant ¾ tsp. baking powder. Fill the container to the ¾-cup mark with water and mix the ingredients together. Add the mixture in place of the eggs. Increase the amount of Baking Mix to 2 ⅜ cups and decrease the flour to ⅝ cup.

Preheat the oven to 350°. Grease one 9- x 13-inch baking pan or two 8- or 9-inch cake pans. Set aside.

In stand mixer fitted with the paddle attachment, measure the oil, brown sugar, and eggs. Beat the mixture on medium speed until blended.

Add the crushed pineapple, Pancake and Baking Mix, flour, and cinnamon. Mix the ingredients on low until the flour is moistened. Then turn the speed to medium until the batter is well blended. Turn off the mixer and scrape down the sides and bottom of the bowl. Add the carrots and nuts and mix again.

Pour the batter into the prepared baking pan(s), and level with a rubber spatula. Bake the 9- x 13-inch pan for 45–50 minutes. If using two 8- or 9-inch layers, bake the cake for 38–43 minutes. The cake is done when a toothpick inserted in the center comes out clean and the cake springs back when lightly pressed in the center.

When the cake is done, allow the pan to cool on a cooling rack for 10 minutes. The 9- x 13-inch cake may remain in the pan. If you have made two 8- or 9-inch layers, remove the cake from the pans and allow them to cool completely.

When the cake is completely cool, frost it with buttercream frosting.

GINGER-PEAR UPSIDE DOWN CAKE

Makes one 9-inch round cake

Ginger and pears team up for a great flavor combination in this moist cake.

Topping
- ¼ cup salted butter, dairy-free margarine, or coconut oil
- ⅓ cup brown sugar
- 2 ripe pears, peeled, core removed, and cut into fourths

Cake
- 1 cup Pancake and Baking Mix
- ½ cup gluten-free oatmeal flour or other substitute from p. 2
- ¾ cup dark brown sugar
- 1 Tbsp. ground ginger
- ½ cup canola oil or other oil of choice

1 cup water
¼ cup egg (1–2 eggs) or egg whites*

Preheat the oven to 400°. Spray a 9-inch round cake pan with nonstick coating. Set aside.

In a small saucepan, combine all the topping ingredients except the pears. Heat and stir over medium heat until the butter melts. Pour the mixture into a greased cake pan. Place the eight pear quarters, rounded side down, in a pretty pattern overtop the brown sugar mixture.

Combine the Pancake and Baking Mix and flour in a medium-sized mixing bowl, then add all the remaining ingredients, adding the liquid last. Stir with a large spoon until well blended. Pour the cake batter carefully over the pears.

Bake for 28–33 minutes or until the top of the cake is firm and springs back when gently pressed.

Remove the cake from the oven and let it sit on a cooling rack for 15 minutes. Invert the cake onto serving plate and serve warm or cold.

Note

Gluten-free cake that contains fruit tends to get soggy after twenty-four hours. To avoid this when storing leftovers, simply press a sheet of plastic wrap against the cut edges to keep them from drying out, but leave the rest of the cake uncovered. Do not put a cover on this cake.

BUTTERCREAM FROSTING

Makes about 2 ½ cups

Homemade frosting is easy to prepare, tastes fabulous, and is so much cheaper than buying a mix.

½ cup salted butter, dairy-free margarine, or coconut oil
1 tsp. vanilla extract
4 cups powdered sugar
¼ cup dairy or non-dairy milk

Measure all the ingredients into a small mixing bowl and blend on low speed. Turn the speed to high and whip for about 30 seconds until the frosting

---

* To replace the eggs, measure 1 Tbsp. cornstarch, tapioca flour, or potato starch into a liquid measure. Add a scant ¼ tsp. baking powder. Fill the container to the ¼-cup mark with water and mix the ingredients together. Add the mixture in place of the eggs. Increase the amount of Baking Mix to 1 ⅛ cups and decrease the flour to ⅜ cup.

Bake the pie until it is bubbly in the center and golden brown on top, approximately 45–55 minutes. Allow the pie to cool for 30 minutes before serving.

VANILLA PUDDING

Makes about 3 ½ cups

This pudding is egg-free, and may be prepared with dairy or non-dairy milk. One recipe yields enough to make one 9-inch vanilla cream pie.

3 cups dairy or non-dairy milk
6 Tbsp. granulated sugar
scant ¼ tsp. salt
1 ½ tsp. unflavored gelatin
2 Tbsp. cornstarch or tapioca flour
4 tsp. of one of the following: white rice flour (gluten-free); spelt flour (wheat-free, but not gluten-free); or all-purpose flour (contains wheat and gluten)
3 Tbsp. salted butter, dairy-free margarine, or coconut oil
2 tsp. vanilla extract

Pour the milk into a medium-sized saucepan with a thick bottom. Measure the sugar, salt, gelatin, cornstarch, and flour into a small bowl and stir together with a fork. Sprinkle the sugar and cornstarch mixture over the milk and whisk the mixture until it is blended.

Place the saucepan on the stove and turn the heat to medium-high. Whisk the mixture constantly until it comes to a boil and thickens. Remove the pan from the heat. Stir in the butter and vanilla and immediately pour the pudding into a serving bowl or individual dessert cups. Let the pudding chill and set up in the refrigerator for several hours or overnight.

Variations:
- **Banana pudding:** Slice three bananas and stir the slices into the slightly warm pudding.
- **Butterscotch pudding:** Substitute 6 Tbsp. brown sugar for the granulated sugar.
- **Coconut pudding:** Stir in ¾ cup toasted flake coconut. (To toast coconut yourself, sprinkle the coconut flakes over a baking sheet and bake in a 350°-oven for about 5–7 minutes, stirring occasionally.) When serving, garnish each dish with more toasted coconut.

- **Maple pudding:** Add ¾ tsp. maple extract and garnish the chilled pudding with finely chopped walnuts.
- **Eggnog pudding:** Add ½ tsp. nutmeg to the pudding and garnish it with more nutmeg before serving.

BERRY CRISP

Makes 9- x 13-inch baking pan

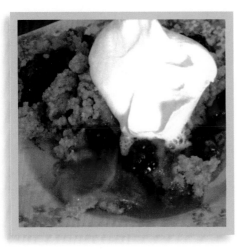

I used blackberries, but any fresh or frozen berry, or tart pie cherries, may be used to make this crisp.

Fruit filling
8 cups blackberries (any fresh or frozen berry of choice may be used)
1 cup granulated sugar
2 Tbsp. cornstarch or tapioca flour
¼ tsp. cinnamon

Oatmeal crisp topping
    ½ cup old fashioned or certified gluten-free oatmeal
    ½ cup brown sugar
    choose one of the following:
        ¼ cup Pancake and Baking Mix plus ¼ cup flour, for a total of ½ cup (gluten-free)
        ½ cup spelt flour plus ⅛ tsp. salt (wheat-free, but not gluten-free)
        ½ cup all-purpose flour plus ⅛ tsp. salt (contains wheat and gluten)
    2 Tbsp. coconut oil or other oil of choice

Preheat the oven to 350° degrees.

Measure the berries into a large bowl. Mix the sugar, cornstarch, and cinnamon in a small bowl and then pour it over the berries. Toss to coat the berries. Transfer to an ungreased 9- x 13-inch baking pan.

Place all the crisp topping ingredients in a medium-sized mixing bowl. Mix the ingredients with a fork until the oil is evenly distributed and then sprinkle the topping over the fruit filling.

Place the uncovered baking dish in a preheated oven, and bake it until golden brown and bubbling, 55 to 60 minutes. Let it cool for 10 minutes before serving. Serve with vanilla non-dairy ice cream.

Variation

- Apple berry crisp: Substitute 3 cups of peeled and sliced apples for 3 cups of the berries.

PECAN PIE

Makes one 9-inch pie

This pie is very allergy friendly. There are no eggs and no corn syrup, but the taste and texture are not compromised in the slightest! Those who may not eat pecans could use pumpkin seeds or raisins.

one recipe No-Roll Pie Crust, 9 inch,
    bottom crust only (see p. 61)
1 ¼ cups cool water
3 Tbsp. cornstarch or tapioca flour
1 package (2 ¼ tsp.) unflavored gelatin
1 ¾ cups brown sugar
3 Tbsp. salted butter, coconut oil, or oil of choice
¼ tsp. salt
2 tsp. vanilla extract
1 ⅓ cups pecans (halves or pieces, according to your preference)

Preheat the oven to 350°.

Prepare the pie crust according to the recipe directions and press the mixture into a 9-inch pie plate; crimp the edges. Bake for 15 minutes. Remove the crust from the oven and set it aside. (This crust does not need to cool before the filling is added.)

Turn the oven down to 275°.

Measure the water into a two-quart saucepan and whisk in the cornstarch and unflavored gelatin. Add the brown sugar, butter, and salt. Stir the mixture to blend and bring it to a boil over medium heat. Once it comes to a boil, turn the heat down to medium-low and allow the mixture to simmer for 3 minutes. Remove the saucepan from the heat and stir in the vanilla and pecans. Pour the filling into the prebaked pie crust.

Bake the pie for one hour and allow it to cool on the counter overnight. Do not refrigerate this pie, or it will be very difficult to cut. Since the pie does not contain eggs, it needs no refrigeration. Also, this pie melts in the microwave, so serve it at room temperature or warm it for a few minutes in a 200° oven.

PECAN PIE (CONTAINS EGGS, BUT NO CORN SYRUP)

one recipe No-Roll Pie Crust, 9 inch, bottom crust only, prepared and
    pre-baked as in the recipe above
¾ cup eggs, egg whites, or liquid egg substitute
1 ⅓ cups pecans (halves or pieces, according to your preference)
2 tsp. vanilla extract
½ cup cool water
1 ¾ cups brown sugar
⅛ tsp. salt
3 Tbsp. salted butter, coconut oil, or oil of choice, at room temperature

Prepare and pre-bake the pie crust as in the recipe above. Turn the oven down to 275°.

Measure the eggs, pecans, and vanilla into a medium-sized mixing bowl and beat the ingredients together with a wooden spoon. Set the mixture aside.

Measure the water, brown sugar, and salt into a two-quart saucepan. Whisk the ingredients to blend them together and allow them to come to a boil over medium heat. Once it comes to a boil, turn it down to medium-low heat and simmer for 3 minutes. Remove the saucepan from the heat.

Beat the pecan mixture with a wooden spoon while slowly adding ½ cup of the hot syrup until well blended. Then pour the pecan mixture into the remaining hot syrup and beat it quickly to incorporate. Continue beating the mixture for about 10 seconds after all the hot syrup has been added. Stir in the butter until it is all melted.

Pour the mixture into the pre-baked pie crust. Bake the pie for 1 hour. Allow it to cool completely before serving. Leftovers may be stored in the refrigerator.

Variations (for both recipes above):
- **Bourbon pecan pie:** When making the filling, decrease the water by 1 ½ Tbsp. When the filling has finished simmering, add 1 ½ Tbsp. of bourbon at the same time pecans are added.
- **Raisin pie:** Replace the pecans with 1 ⅓ cups raisins.
- **Rum raisin pie:** When making the filling, decrease the water by 1 ½ Tbsp. When the filling has finished simmering, add 1 ½ Tbsp. rum at the same time the raisins are added. A second option is to replace 1 tsp. vanilla extract with 1 tsp. rum extract.

PART FIVE

COOKIES, CANDIES, AND SNACKS

FUDGE

Makes one 8- x 8-inch pan of nut-free fudge or one 9- x 9-inch pan of fudge with nuts

This recipe for creamy fudge is not only easy to make, but it may also be prepared dairy-free!

1 Tbsp. unflavored gelatin
1 ¼ cups dairy or non-dairy milk
¾ cup baking cocoa
1 cup coconut oil (or oil of preference)
3 cups granulated sugar
¼ tsp. salt
½ tsp. vanilla extract
1 cup walnuts, nuts of choice, or dried fruit (optional)

Lightly grease one 8- x 8-inch or 9- x 9-inch pan with butter or vegetable shortening. Set aside.

Dissolve the gelatin in cold milk. Measure the cocoa, coconut oil, sugar, and salt into a sturdy four-quart saucepan. Add the milk-gelatin mixture. Turn the heat to medium and stir the fudge with wooden spoon, scraping the bottom and sides of pan, until the coconut oil is melted and all the ingredients are blended. Attach a candy thermometer to the side of the pan, being sure the end of the thermometer is not touching the bottom of the pan.

Stir from time to time until the fudge comes to a boil. Turn heat down to medium-low and simmer, without stirring, for 15 minutes. The temperature will climb to 225° and will stay there. Remove from heat and add vanilla and walnuts; stir to incorporate.

Let the pan cool for 15 minutes if nuts were added and for 30 minutes if it is nut-free. (The nuts cool down the fudge, so it will be ready sooner.) Beat the cooled fudge with a wooden spoon for 5 minutes until it is very thick and shiny.

Spread the fudge into the prepared pan and smooth it with a spatula. Place the fudge in the refrigerator until it gets firm and cut it into 1-inch squares. A metal spatula is perfect for lifting the fudge out of the pan.

CARAMEL CRUNCH APPLES

Makes two apple halves

1 apple, cut in half, stemmed and
   cored
2 Tbsp. brown sugar
¼ tsp. nutmeg or cloves
One of the following kinds of flour:
   3 Tbsp. Pancake and Baking
      Mix plus 3 Tbsp. gluten-free
      oatmeal flour or other substi-
      tute from p. 2 (gluten-free)
   6 Tbsp. spelt flour (wheat-free, but
      not gluten-free)
   6 Tbsp. all-purpose or whole wheat flour (contains wheat and gluten)
2 Tbsp. salted butter, dairy-free margarine, or coconut oil
one recipe Caramel Sauce (see p. 129)

Preheat the oven to 350°. Place two apple halves, cut side up, in a small baking pan. Mix together the brown sugar, nutmeg, and flour. Rub the butter into the dry ingredients with your fingers. Pack the apple halves with the crumb topping and place them in the oven.

Bake the apples until they are tender and the crumb topping is golden brown, about 30–35 minutes. If the tops brown too quickly, gently lay a small piece of foil over the apples and continue baking until the apples are soft.

Let the apples cool until they are lukewarm. Place the apple halves in two small dessert bowls. Top with dairy-free ice cream or whipping cream and drizzle caramel sauce over the top.

PEANUT-FREE PEANUT BRITTLE

Makes one 9- x 13-inch pan

My grandma's yummy peanut brittle recipe is now allergy-friendly! I used raw pumpkin and sunflower seeds in place of peanuts. If you can eat peanuts, replace all the seeds with 3 cups raw peanuts.

It is a good idea to pre-measure the seeds, oil and salt, and baking soda into separate bowls and place them next to the stove so they will be easy to access while you are cooking the peanut brittle.

1 ½ cups raw pumpkin seeds
1 ½ cups raw sunflower seeds
1 Tbsp. coconut oil or other oil of choice
¼ tsp. salt
2 ½ tsp. baking soda
2 cups granulated sugar
1 cup brown rice syrup or white corn syrup
½ cup water

Thoroughly grease a 9- x 13-inch pan, going halfway up the sides of the pan.

Measure the sugar, brown rice syrup, and water into a three-quart saucepan and stir to blend. Attach a candy thermometer to the side of the pan, and be sure it is not touching the bottom.

Bring the mixture to a boil quickly over high heat. Do not stir it until it reaches 240°. (If you are not at sea level but at 3,000 feet, it would need to reach 235°.) Add the pumpkin and sunflower seeds. Turn the heat down to medium and stir the mixture frequently until it reaches 295° or until the syrup turns an amber color. (At 3,000 feet, allow it to reach 290°.)

Remove the candy from the heat and immediately stir in the coconut oil and salt. Beat in the baking soda and quickly pour the hot brittle into the prepared 9- x 13-inch pan. Scrape out the saucepan with a heat-resistant spatula. Spread the brittle evenly in the pan. Set the pan aside to cool for 45–60 minutes or until it is room temperature.

Tip the peanut brittle pan upside down and shake it until the brittle falls out. Gently hit the back of the brittle with small hammer to break it into pieces. Put the brittle in a candy dish to serve it.

MICROWAVE POPCORN

Makes 2 quarts

There's nothing artificial here, just natural corn flavor. Adding the salt to the oil gives the popcorn a really nice flavor.

3 Tbsp. coconut oil or other oil of choice
1 tsp. salt
⅓ cup popcorn

Measure the oil, salt, and popcorn into a microwavable four-quart casserole dish and cover the dish with a lid. Put it in the microwave and cook on high 1 minute to melt the coconut oil. Swish the dish to coat the popcorn with oil and salt.

Cook the popcorn 5 ½ minutes longer or until most of popcorn has popped. (Cooking times will vary depending on your microwave, so keep an eye on it, adding or subtracting time as needed.)

Use a potholder to lift the casserole dish from the microwave. Remove the lid so that the popcorn does not become soggy. Sprinkle the popcorn with additional salt to taste.

Variation
• "Parmesan" popcorn: Sprinkle ¼ cup nutritional yeast over the popped popcorn.

BISCOTTI WITH ANISE

Makes 2 dozen cookies

Make the biscotti as strong or as mild as you would like by adjusting the amount of anise.

1 cup salted butter, coconut oil, vegetable shortening, or lard (if butter is not used, add ¼ tsp. salt)
1 cup granulated sugar
¾ cup eggs (3–4 eggs) or egg whites*
1 tsp. vanilla extract
2–4 tsp. anise seeds (to taste)
2 cups Pancake and Baking Mix
2 ¼ cups gluten-free oatmeal flour or other substitute from p. 2

Preheat the oven to 350°. Set out one large cookie sheet (do not grease it).

In a stand mixer fitted with the paddle attachment, blend the butter and sugar on medium speed until well blended. Add the eggs, vanilla, and anise seeds. Blend again until the batter is smooth. Turn off the mixer and add Pancake and Baking Mix and flour. Blend on low until all the ingredients are thoroughly combined. Turn off the mixer and scrape down the sides and bottom of the mixing bowl. Mix the dough again until all the ingredients are well blended.

Divide the dough in half and shape each portion into a log 6 inches long and 1 ½ inches across. Place the logs a few inches apart on the baking sheet. Bake the biscotti in the oven for 30 minutes.

Remove the cookie logs from the oven and, using a serrated knife, gently slice each log into twelve cookies. They should each be ¾ inch thick. Place each cookie cut-side down, side-by-side on the baking sheet.

Return the cookies to the oven and bake for an additional 15 minutes until the side touching the cookie sheet is golden brown. Remove the cookies from the oven.

Using a metal spatula, carefully turn each cookie over. Return the pan to the oven and bake 15 minutes longer, until the bottom side is golden brown.

---

* To replace the eggs, measure 3 Tbsp. cornstarch, tapioca flour, or potato starch into a liquid measure. Add a scant ½ tsp. baking powder. Fill the container to the ¾-cup mark with water and mix the ingredients together. Add the mixture in place of the eggs. Increase the amount of Baking Mix to 2 ⅜ cups and decrease the flour to 1 ⅞ cups.

Remove the cookies from the oven and use a metal spatula to move each cookie to a cooling rack. Allow the biscotti to cool completely.

CHOCOLATE CHIP COOKIES

Makes about 4 dozen cookies

These gluten-free cookies are just as tasty and tender as any "regular" chocolate chip cookie!

½ cup vegetable shortening
½ cup salted butter, coconut oil, or
   dairy-free margarine
1 ½ cups brown sugar
½ cup eggs (2–3 eggs) or egg
   whites*
4 tsp. vanilla extract
1 ½ cups Pancake and Baking Mix
1 ¼ cups gluten-free oatmeal flour or other substitute from p. 2
1 cup chopped walnuts or pecans (optional)
10–12 oz. (1 ¼ to 1 ½ cups) allergy-free or semi-sweet chocolate chips

Preheat the oven to 350°. Lightly grease cookie sheets, or line with parchment paper; set aside.

In a stand mixer fitted with the paddle attachment, blend the shortening, butter, and brown sugar on medium speed. Add the eggs and vanilla and mix thoroughly. Turn off the mixer and add all the remaining ingredients except the walnuts and chocolate chips. Mix on low until all the ingredients are moistened, and then turn the mixer to medium speed. Once the dough is evenly blended, stop mixer and scrape down the sides and bottom of the mixing bowl. Mix the dough again until it is smooth. Stir in the walnuts and chocolate chips.

Using a 1 ½ Tbsp. cookie scoop, make balls of dough and place them about 2 inches apart on the prepared baking sheet. (If using a ⅛ cup cookie scoop, the baking time will need to be increased by 1–2 minutes.)

Bake the cookies for 11–13 minutes or until they are just starting to turn brown. Remove the cookies from oven and allow them to cool on baking sheet for about 2 minutes. Lift the cookies from the baking sheet using a spatula.

* To replace the eggs, measure 2 Tbsp. cornstarch, tapioca flour, or potato starch into a liquid measure. Add ¼ tsp. baking powder. Fill the container to the ½-cup mark with water and mix the ingredients together. Add the mixture in place of the eggs. Increase the amount of Baking Mix to 1 ¾ cups and decrease the flour to 1 cup.

OATMEAL RAISIN COOKIES

Makes about 4 dozen cookies

½ cup vegetable shortening or lard
½ cup salted butter, coconut oil, or
  dairy-free margarine
1 ½ cups brown sugar
½ cup eggs (2–3 eggs) or egg
  whites*
2 Tbsp. dairy or non-dairy milk
2 tsp. vanilla extract
¾ cup Pancake and Baking Mix
⅜ cup gluten-free oatmeal flour or
  other substitute from p. 2

4 tsp. cinnamon
3 cups certified gluten-free oats (those who may eat gluten should use
  quick-cooking oats)
1 cup chopped walnuts (optional)
1 cup raisins

Preheat the oven to 350°. Lightly grease the cookie sheets or line them with parchment paper; set aside.

In a stand mixer fitted with the paddle attachment, blend shortening, butter, and brown sugar on medium speed. Add the eggs, milk, and vanilla; blend on low. Turn off the mixer and add all the remaining ingredients except the walnuts and raisins. Continue to mix the dough on low until all the ingredients are moistened, then turn the mixer to medium speed. When the dough is well blended, stop the mixer and scrape down the sides and bottom of the mixing bowl. Mix the dough again until it looks smooth. Stir in the walnuts and raisins.

Using a 1 ½ Tbsp. cookie scoop, make balls of dough and place them about 2 inches apart on the prepared baking sheet. (If using a ⅛ cup cookie scoop, the baking time will need to be increased by 1–2 minutes.) Bake the cookies for 11–13 minutes, or until they are just starting to get brown. When they are done, remove them from the oven and allow them to cool on a baking sheet for about 2 minutes.

---

* To replace the eggs, measure 2 Tbsp. cornstarch, tapioca flour, or potato starch into a liquid measure. Add ¼ tsp. baking powder. Fill the container to the ½-cup mark with water and mix the ingredients together. Add the mixture in place of the eggs. Increase the amount of Baking Mix to 1 cup and decrease the flour to ⅛ cup.

SNICKERDOODLES

Makes about 3 ½ dozen cookies

I actually like these gluten-free Snickerdoodles better than those that contain gluten!

Also pictured: No-Roll Sugar Cookes

2 Tbsp. granulated sugar
4 tsp. cinnamon
½ cup vegetable shortening or lard
½ cup salted butter, coconut oil, or dairy-free margarine
1 ½ cups granulated sugar
½ cup eggs (2–3 eggs) or egg whites*
1 ⅓ cups Pancake and Baking Mix
1 cup gluten-free oatmeal flour or other substitute from p. 2

Preheat the oven to 350°. Grease two baking sheets (or line with parchment paper), and set aside.

In a small bowl, combine 2 Tbsp. sugar and 4 tsp. cinnamon. Set aside.

In a stand mixer fitted with the paddle attachment, blend the shortening, butter, and 1 ½ cups sugar on medium speed. Add the eggs and blend again. Turn off the mixer and add the Pancake and Baking Mix and flour. Blend the ingredients on low until just moistened, and then turn the mixer to medium speed. Stop the mixer when the dough is well blended and scrape down the sides and bottom of the mixing bowl. Mix the dough again until it is smooth.

Using a 1 ½ Tbsp. cookie scoop, make balls of dough. (If you are using a ⅛ cup cookie scoop, the baking time will need to be increased by 1–2 minutes.) Roll the dough balls in the cinnamon-sugar mixture and place the cookies 2-inches apart on a prepared cookie sheet.

Bake the cookies for 11–13 minutes or until they just start to brown. Remove the pan from the oven and allow the cookies to cool on the baking sheet for about 2 minutes.

* To replace the eggs, measure 2 Tbsp. cornstarch, tapioca flour, or potato starch into a liquid measure. Add ¼ tsp. baking powder. Fill the container to the ½-cup mark with water and mix the ingredients together. Add the mixture in place of the eggs. Increase the amount of Baking Mix to 1 ½ cups plus 1 Tbsp. and decrease the flour to ¾ cup.

No-Roll Sugar Cookies

Makes about 4 dozen cookies

These cookies have a crisp texture and fabulous flavor.

1 ⅓ cups granulated sugar, divided
½ cup vegetable shortening or lard
½ cup salted butter, coconut oil, or dairy-free margarine
1 cup powdered sugar
½ cup eggs (2–3 eggs) or egg whites[*]
1 cup canola oil or other oil of choice
4 tsp. vanilla extract
1 Tbsp. almond or lemon extract
1 ½ cups Pancake and Baking Mix
1 ½ cups gluten-free oatmeal flour or other substitute from p. 2

Preheat the oven to 350°. Grease two baking sheets (or line with parchment paper) and set aside.

Measure ⅓ cup sugar into a small bowl and set aside.

In a stand mixer fitted with the paddle attachment, blend 1 cup sugar, shortening, butter, and powdered sugar on medium speed. Add eggs, oil, vanilla, and almond extract; blend again. Turn off the mixer and add the Pancake and Baking Mix and flour. Blend the ingredients on low until just moistened, then turn the mixer to medium speed until all the ingredients are well blended. Stop the mixer and scrape down the sides and bottom of the mixing bowl. Mix the dough again until it is smooth.

Using a 1 ½ Tbsp. cookie scoop, make balls of dough and place them about 2 inches apart on the prepared baking sheet. (If you are using a ⅛ cup cookie scoop, the baking time will need to be increased by 1–2 minutes.)

Dip a moistened drinking glass with a flat, wide bottom into the bowl of sugar. Press the first cookie to a ¼ inch thickness. Dip the drinking glass back into the sugar and then press the next cookie. Repeat the process until all the cookies have been pressed to a ¼-inch thickness.

Bake the cookies for 10–12 minutes or until the cookies are just starting to brown. Remove them from the oven and allow them to cool on a baking sheet for about 2 minutes before lifting them onto a cooling rack with a metal spatula.

---

[*] To replace the eggs, measure 2 Tbsp. cornstarch, tapioca flour, or potato starch into a liquid measure. Add ¼ tsp. baking powder. Fill the container to the ½-cup mark with water and mix the ingredients together. Add the mixture in place of the eggs. Increase the amount of Baking Mix to 1 ¾ cups and decrease the flour to 1 ¼ cups.

Raisin Bars

Anyone who likes raisins will
love these!

Crust
1 cup Pancake and Baking Mix
⅔ cup gluten-free oatmeal flour or
    other substitute from p. 2
¼ cup granulated sugar
¾ cup salted butter, coconut oil, or
    vegetable shortening (if butter is
    not used, add a scant ¼ tsp. salt)

Raisin filling
1 ½ cups brown sugar
1 ½ Tbsp. cornstarch, tapioca flour, or potato starch
1 cup eggs, egg whites, or liquid egg substitute
2 tsp. vanilla extract
2 ½ cups raisins

Preheat the oven to 350°.

To prepare the crust, combine the Pancake and Baking Mix, flour, and sugar in a small mixing bowl. Add the butter, and rub the butter into the dry ingredients using your fingers. Press the mixture into an ungreased 9- x 13-inch baking pan. Bake for 15 minutes. Remove the pan from the oven and set aside. (This crust does not need to cool before the filling is added.)

Turn the oven to 275° and begin to work on the filling.

Measure the brown sugar, cornstarch, eggs, and vanilla into a medium-sized metal bowl and beat the ingredients together with a wooden spoon. Stir in the raisins and pour the mixture into the prepared crust. Spread the filling evenly over the crust.

Bake the raisin bars for 23–27 minutes or until the top is lightly browned. Place the pan on a cooling rack until the bars come to room temperature. Using a very sharp knife or a pizza cutter, cut the pan into twenty-four bars. They are best served at room temperature.

Egg-free Raisin Bars

To make the raisin filling without eggs, substitute the ingredients in the recipe above with the following:

1 ¼ cups cool water
3 Tbsp. cornstarch, potato starch, or tapioca flour
2 tsp. unflavored gelatin
1 ¾ cups brown sugar
¼ tsp. salt
2 tsp. vanilla extract
2 ½ cups raisins

Measure the water into a two-quart saucepan. Whisk in the cornstarch and unflavored gelatin. Add the brown sugar and salt and stir to blend. Bring the mixture to a boil over medium heat. Once it comes to a boil, turn the heat to medium-low and let it simmer for 3 minutes. Remove the pan from heat and add the vanilla and raisins. Stir the filling and pour it over the crust, being careful to spread it evenly.

Bake the raisin bars for 23–27 minutes or until the top is lightly browned.

Variations

- **Rum-raisin bars:** Reduce the vanilla to 1 tsp. and add 1 tsp. rum extract.
- **Pecan pie bars:** Substitute 2 ½ cups pecans for raisins when making the raisin filling (either with or without eggs).
- **Bourbon pecan pie bars:** This only works in the egg-free version of the raisin filling. Substitute 2 ½ cups pecans for raisins. When making the filling, use only 1 cup plus 3 Tbsp. cool water. Once the mixture has finished boiling, add 1 Tbsp. bourbon at the same time the vanilla and pecans are added.

Fudge Brownies

Makes a 9- x 13-inch pan

2 Tbsp. dairy or non-dairy milk
⅞ cup canola oil or other oil of choice
2 ¼ cups granulated sugar
1 Tbsp. vanilla extract

MAIN DISHES

Also pictured: Barbeque Chicken with Pineapple Pizza, Chipotle Chicken Pizza

MEAT AND VEGETABLE PIZZA

Makes one 12- x 16-inch jellyroll pan or one round pizza pan

If there is no cheese substitute available, make the pizza without cheese.
It still tastes great!

one recipe Focaccia Bread (see p. 28)
one recipe Pizza Sauce (see p. 123)
¾ cup of one of the following: chopped onion, chopped mushrooms, chopped arti-
  choke hearts
2 cups of either ground beef, ground turkey, chicken, or ham, cooked and chopped
1 cup of one of the following: green peppers, sliced in short strips; sliced black
  olives; pineapple chunks; sauerkraut, drained
8 oz. rice mozzarella cheese or other cheese of choice
2 tsp. dried parsley

Preheat the oven to 425°.

Prepare the focaccia bread dough according to the recipe directions. Press the dough into a pizza or jellyroll pan. Prepare the sauce and pour it over the focaccia bread, spreading the sauce over the entire surface of the dough. Sprinkle the toppings over the sauce, adding the cheese and parsley last.

Bake the pizza for 25–30 minutes or until the bottom of the crust is done and all the vegetables are tender. Remove the pizza from the oven and cut it with pizza cutter.

BARBECUE CHICKEN WITH PINEAPPLE PIZZA

Makes one 12- x 16-inch jellyroll pan or one round pizza pan

Now, this is a treat!

one recipe Focaccia Bread (see p. 28)
2 cups Barbecue Sauce (see p. 122)
2 cups cooked chicken, cut into bite-sized chunks
1 medium red onion, sliced thin and caramelized
8 oz. pineapple slices in their own juice, drained and cut into bite-sized
    pieces
3 Tbsp. feta cheese (optional)
8 oz. (or 2 ⅔ cups) rice mozzarella cheese or other cheese of choice
    (optional)
¼ cup fresh cilantro leaves, for the garnish

Follow the directions for the meat and vegetable pizza, and garnish with cilantro leaves just before serving.

CHIPOTLE CHICKEN PIZZA

Makes one 12- x 16-inch jellyroll pan or one round pizza pan

This pizza can be served mild or fire cracker hot, depending on how much chipotle sauce is used!

one recipe Focaccia Bread (see p. 28)
¼ cup Chipotle Sauce (see p. 124)
1 ¾ cups Barbecue Sauce (see p. 122)
2 cups cooked chicken, cut into bite-sized chunks, or cooked ground beef
    (about 10 oz.)
¾ cup chopped onions or sliced mushrooms, tomatoes, or bell pepper
    (your choice)

3.8 oz. sliced black olives
8 oz. (2 ⅔ cups) rice mozzarella cheese or other cheese of choice
  (optional)

Follow the directions for the meat and vegetable pizza to assemble and bake. If you want a spicier pizza, increase the amount of chipotle sauce. The amount of chipotle sauce plus barbecue sauce should still equal 2 cups total.

OVEN-FRIED CHICKEN WITH ROASTED POTATOES

Serves 4

Let the oven do the work!

3 lbs. chicken pieces (bone-in and skin-on has the best flavor and stays moist while baking)
½ cup gluten-free oatmeal or other substitute from p. 2
½ tsp. salt
¼ tsp. pepper
¼ tsp. garlic powder
½ tsp. poultry seasoning
2 baking potatoes, cut in half lengthwise

Preheat the oven to 350°.
Rinse the chicken pieces and drain them. Mix the flour, salt, pepper, garlic powder, and poultry seasoning in a pie plate. Coat each piece of chicken in the flour mixture and arrange the pieces in a single layer on a large ungreased jelly-roll pan. Place the potatoes on the same jellyroll pan cut-side down in a single layer. (They will not stick.)
Place the baking pan in the oven without a cover and set the timer for one hour. Neither the chicken nor potatoes need to be turned while they are baking. At the end of the baking time, remove the pan from the oven and turn on the broiler. Turn potatoes over, so they are cut-side up. Place the oven rack at the highest position and broil the chicken and potatoes for 4–8 minutes with the door slightly ajar, until the chicken and potatoes are golden brown. Watch them carefully so they do not burn, moving the pan as needed so all the pieces brown evenly.

Lasagna Casserole

Serves 10-12

12 oz. (about 4 ¾ cups) brown rice
  spiral pasta, or 12 oz. of another
  pasta of your choice, any shape
1 ½ Tbsp. olive oil or oil of choice
¾ cup chopped onion (or 2 Tbsp.
  dried flake onions)
1 lb. extra-lean ground beef or
  turkey
2 cloves garlic, minced
1 Tbsp. dried basil
1 ½ tsp. fennel seed
¾ tsp. dried thyme
¾ tsp. dried oregano
⅛ tsp. red chili flakes or black pepper
3 Tbsp. dried parsley
28 oz. diced or stewed tomatoes
8 oz. tomato sauce
1 cup grated mozzarella cheese or cheese substitute (optional)

Cook the pasta according to the package directions. Drain the pasta in a colander and rinse it quickly with cold water.

While the pasta is cooking, prepare the meat sauce. Place a four-quart saucepan over medium heat and add oil. Fry the onion, hamburger, and all spices together for 7–8 minutes or until the hamburger is lightly browned. Add the canned tomatoes and tomato sauce. Simmer the sauce uncovered over low heat for 15 minutes.

Add the cheese and pasta. Cook for 1–2 minutes or until it is heated through, stirring as necessary so the pasta does not stick to bottom of pan.

BARBECUED PORK RIBS

Serves 4

My mom used to make this when I was growing up, and it was always one of my favorite dishes. The slow cooking makes the meat super tender.

This recipe is also great with chicken pieces or boneless sirloin pork chops instead of ribs.

2 lbs. pork ribs
1 large onion, peeled and sliced
⅓ cup ketchup
⅔ cup water
1 Tbsp. minced garlic
½ tsp. salt
¼ tsp. black pepper
¼ tsp. dry mustard
¼ tsp. chili powder
¼ tsp. cayenne pepper or hot red pepper sauce
1 scant Tbsp. molasses or brown sugar

Preheat the oven to 350°. *250°*

Arrange a layer of ribs in a four-quart casserole dish with a snug-fitting lid. Top the ribs with a layer of half the sliced onions. Make a second layer of ribs and then a second layer of onions.

Mix all the remaining ingredients in a small mixing bowl and pour the mixture over the ribs. Place the lid on the casserole dish and place it in the oven. Bake it for three hours or until the meat is tender.

Herb-Roasted Chicken with Roast Potatoes and Gravy

Serves 4-6 people

The flavor of the spices makes this chicken "finger-licking good." This recipe is for a whole chicken; the variation of this recipe to use for individual chicken pieces is on page 94.

one whole 4-lb. chicken
2 tsp. salt
½ tsp. black pepper
1 ¼ tsp. dried thyme
1 ¼ tsp. dried basil
1 ¼ tsp. dried rosemary
2 Tbsp. canola oil or oil of choice
3–4 large baking potatoes, washed and cut in half lengthwise

Gravy
Drippings from chicken plus enough cold water to make 1 cup
1 Tbsp. cornstarch or potato starch
salt and pepper to taste

Preheat the oven to 350°. Remove the giblets from the cavity of the chicken. Rinse the chicken inside and out and blot it dry with a paper towel. Place the chicken breast-side up on an ungreased 17- x 15-inch roasting pan (or similar sized jelly roll pan). Place the potatoes cut-side down in a single layer surrounding the chicken.

In a small bowl, mix the spices and oil. Rub the inside cavity of the chicken with 1 Tbsp. of the oil and spice mixture. Rub the outside with the remaining oil and spice mixture.

Place the chicken in the oven without a cover. Bake for 90–100 minutes and then check for doneness. When the chicken is done the juices will run clear and the meat will come off the bones easily.

To make the gravy, pour the drippings into a liquid measure and add enough cold water to make 1 cup. Whisk in 1 Tbsp. cornstarch. Heat the gravy over medium heat on the stovetop, whisking from time to time until it comes to a boil and thickens. Remove the pan from heat and serve it over the potatoes.

Variation

- **Herb-roasted chicken pieces:** Arrange 3 lbs. of chicken pieces of choice (bone-in and skin-on) in a jellyroll pan. Mix 1 ½ tsp. salt, ½ tsp. black pepper, 1 tsp. dried thyme, 1 tsp. dried basil, and 1 tsp. dried rosemary. Sprinkle the mixture over the chicken pieces and bake them at 350° for 60–75 minutes or until the juices run clear.

CAJUN CASSEROLE

Serves 8

2 cups jasmine rice or rice of choice
1 Tbsp. olive oil or oil of choice
1 lb extra-lean ground beef, ground turkey, or boneless and skinless chicken breasts, cut into 1-inch pieces
1 cup chopped yellow onion
1 clove garlic, minced
1 Tbsp. paprika
1 Tbsp. chili powder
2 tsp. dried basil
2 tsp. dried thyme
1 ½ tsp. cumin
1 tsp. dry mustard
14.5 oz. stewed or diced tomatoes, juice and all
4 cups beef or chicken broth
a few shakes hot pepper sauce, to taste

Preheat the oven to 400°. Measure the rice into a four-quart casserole dish with a snugly fitting lid.

In a medium-sized nonstick frying pan heat the oil on medium. Add the ground beef, onion, garlic, and all seasonings. Sauté the mixture for 5–6 minutes or until the hamburger is lightly browned on all sides and the onion is tender. Transfer the meat to the casserole dish and mix it with the rice.

Heat the stewed tomatoes, chicken broth, and hot pepper sauce together in a two-quart saucepan over high heat. When it comes to a boil, pour it over the meat and rice mixture. Stir to distribute the ingredients evenly. Put a snugly fitting lid on the casserole dish and bake it for 40–45 minutes without removing the lid.

At the end of the baking time, remove the casserole from the oven and use a fork to skim off a few of the top grains of rice. If they are tender, the casserole

Tuna Casserole

Serves 4

For a basic tuna fish casserole, omit the celery, water chestnuts, mushrooms, and black olives. However, those extras sure do add a nice touch to this dish!

12 oz. brown rice elbow macaroni (or 12 oz. of another pasta of your choice), cooked and drained
2 Tbsp. olive oil or oil of choice
½ cup chopped green onions
1 cup celery
2 ½ cups dairy or non-dairy milk
1 ½ Tbsp. cornstarch or tapioca flour
1 tsp. salt
¼ tsp. pepper
12 oz. tuna fish, drained
5 oz. sliced water chestnuts, drained
4 oz. sliced mushrooms, drained
3.8 oz. black olives

Preheat the oven to 350°.

In a medium-sized saucepan over medium heat, sauté the green onions and celery in the oil for 5 minutes. Whisk together the milk, cornstarch, salt, and pepper; then add it to the pan with the onions. Cook the mixture until it comes to a boil and thickens. Add the tuna, water chestnuts, mushrooms, and olives. Stir to blend all the ingredients.

Transfer the cooked macaroni to a two-quart casserole dish and pour the tuna gravy over it. Stir to combine, then bake uncovered for 30 minutes, until bubbly.

SHAKE AND THEN BAKE

Serves 4-6

3 lbs. chicken pieces, bone-in and
   skin-on
½ cup cornstarch or tapioca flour
⅝ cup cornmeal, almond meal,
   brown rice flour, or sorghum flour
2 Tbsp. Italian seasoning
1 ½ Tbsp. paprika
1 ½ tsp. onion powder
1 tsp. garlic powder
2 tsp. salt
¼ tsp. black pepper
½ tsp. allspice

Preheat the oven to 350°. Set out a 12- x 16-inch jellyroll pan. Do not grease it.

Rinse off the chicken pieces and place them in colander to drain, but do not pat them dry.

Measure all the remaining ingredients into a zip-top bag. Place two of the chicken pieces into the bag and zip the top shut. Shake the bag a few times to coat the chicken. Open the bag and remove the chicken. Transfer the coated pieces to the jellyroll pan. Repeat the process with the remaining pieces of chicken and arrange them side-by-side on a jellyroll pan.

Place the chicken in the oven and bake for 60 minutes. Check the meat for doneness by cutting into one of the thickest pieces. The meat should be white and the juices should run clear. Serve the chicken while it's hot.

SHAKE AND THEN BAKE MIX (TO MAKE THE MIX IN BULK)

Makes 8 meals using 1 ½ cups mix each time (1 ½ cups will coat 3 lbs. of chicken pieces)

4 cups cornstarch or tapioca flour
5 cups cornmeal, almond meal, brown rice flour, or sorghum flour
1 cup Italian seasoning
¾ cup paprika
4 Tbsp. onion powder
2 Tbsp. plus 2 tsp. garlic powder
5 Tbsp. plus 1 tsp. salt
2 tsp. black pepper
4 tsp. allspice

SHEPHERD'S PIE WITH CARROT MASHED POTATOES

Serves 4

When made with carrot mashed potatoes, this makes a complete meal.

one recipe Carrot Mashed Potatoes
   (see p. 119)
1 Tbsp. canola oil or other oil of
   choice
1 medium onion, chopped
1 clove garlic, minced
1 pound ground beef or turkey
½ tsp. dried thyme
½ tsp. dried basil
½ tsp. poultry seasoning
¼ tsp. black pepper
2 Tbsp. of either brown rice flour, sorghum flour, spelt flour (wheat-free),
   or all-purpose flour (wheat)
1 cup beef broth or broth of choice
1 Tbsp. Worcestershire sauce (read the label to be sure it's allergy-free)
2 Tbsp. ketchup
1 ⅓ cups frozen (thawed) or fresh (pre-cooked) peas, green beans, or
   spinach (any reheated leftover vegetable may be used)

Preheat the oven to 400°.

While the potatoes and carrots are simmering for the carrot mashed potatoes, start cooking the meat. In a medium-sized nonstick frying pan, heat the oil over medium-high heat. Sauté the onions and garlic for 1–2 minutes, then add the ground beef and all the spices. Cook the meat until no pink remains, then turn the heat down to medium.

Add the flour to the pan and turn the meat over and over until the flour is incorporated. Add the next three ingredients and stir the mixture until the gravy thickens.

Put the meat into a two-quart casserole dish and level with a spatula. Sprinkle the peas or green beans over the meat. Spread the mashed potatoes over the top and level with a spatula. Pull the end of a fork carefully across the top surface several times to make a pretty pattern, if desired.

Place the casserole dish in the oven uncovered. Bake the shepherd's pie for 30 minutes, until the top is golden brown and the meat sauce is bubbly. (Instead of baking the casserole for 30 minutes at 400°, another option is to broil the assembled casserole for 4–8 minutes or until the surface of the potatoes are golden brown. Watch it carefully so the casserole does not burn and move the casserole dish as needed so the top browns evenly.)

CRUNCHY TACO CASSEROLE

Serves 8

This is good with or without cheese and may be served as a simple taco casserole without corn (or rice) chips.

2 cups jasmine rice or rice of choice
2 Tbsp. olive oil or oil of choice
1 lb. extra-lean ground beef or
  chicken breast, cut in strips
2 tsp. onion powder
1 tsp. garlic powder
1 Tbsp. chili powder
2 tsp. cumin
1 tsp. Mexican oregano (or oregano)
28–29 oz. stewed or chopped tomatoes
6 oz. sliced black olives, drained
4 cups beef or chicken broth
2–3 cups grated dairy or non-dairy cheddar cheese (optional)
9.25 ounces corn chips (or rice chips)

Preheat the oven to 400°. Measure the rice into a four-quart casserole dish and set aside.

Heat the oil into medium-sized nonstick frying pan over medium heat. Fry the ground beef and all the seasonings. Cook for 5–6 minutes, or until the hamburger is lightly browned on all sides. Add the stewed tomatoes, black olives, and chicken broth; stir it until it comes to a boil. Remove the pan from the heat.

Carefully ladle all the meat and broth into the casserole dish. Stir to blend the meat sauce with the rice and sprinkle the cheese on top. Cover the casserole with a lid and bake it for 50–55 minutes. (If you are using brown rice, increase the cooking time by 15 minutes. It may also need 2–3 additional tablespoonfuls of chicken broth during the last 15 minutes of cooking.)

At the end of the baking time, remove the casserole from the oven and use a fork to skim off a few of the top grains of rice. If they are tender, the casserole is done. All the liquid should be incorporated into the rice. If some liquid still remains, remove the lid and the excess liquid will evaporate in 1–2 minutes.

Sprinkle corn chips over the casserole before serving.

Sweet and Sour Chicken (or Pork)

Serves 4-5

This yummy sauce is free of soy sauce and may be prepared without cornstarch also.

one recipe Sweet and Sour Sauce (see p. 123)
1 medium onion, cut in thin wedges
8 oz. fresh large mushrooms, washed and cut in half
½ green bell pepper, seeded and cut in bite-sized pieces
½ red bell pepper, seeded and cut in bite-sized pieces
2 medium carrots, peeled and cut diagonally in ¼-inch slices
5 oz. sliced water chestnuts, drained
2 tsp. minced garlic
1 lb. boneless skinless chicken breasts (or boneless pork), cut into bite-sized pieces
1 ½ cups jasmine or basmati rice or rice of choice
3 ¼ cups hot water
Canola oil (or other oil of choice) for frying the meat and vegetables

Make the sweet and sour sauce and keep it warm on the stove over low heat. Preheat the oven to 350°.

Measure the rice into a large strainer and hold it under running water to rinse off the starch. Let the rice drain and transfer it to a two-quart casserole dish with a snugly fitting lid. Add 3 ¼ cups hot water, put the lid on the casserole dish, and place it in the oven. Set a timer for 30 minutes. (Brown rice will need to cook for 45 minutes.) When the timer rings, check the rice for doneness by skimming a few rice grains from the top. The grains should be tender. If the rice needs to cook longer, add an additional 2 Tbsp. of hot water and bake for 10 minutes longer. When the rice is done, turn the oven down to 175°, add 2 Tbsp. water (to keep rice from drying out), and keep it warm in the oven until serving time.

Place a medium-sized nonstick frying pan over medium heat. Add 2 Tbsp. oil. Add one of the vegetables and sauté it for 3–5 minutes or until it is tender-crisp. Add salt and pepper to taste. Transfer that vegetable to a four-quart soup kettle. Do not put a lid on the kettle or the vegetables will get soggy. Again, measure 2 Tbsp. oil into the frying pan and add the next vegetable. When they are tender-crisp, season them with salt and pepper to taste and transfer them to the soup kettle. Continue this process until all the vegetables have been cooked, except for the garlic.

Last of all, cook the meat. Heat 2 Tbsp. oil in the frying pan and add the garlic and meat. Cook until the meat is done and the juices run clear. Add the meat to the soup kettle and season the pot with salt and pepper.

Pour warm sweet and sour sauce over all the meat and vegetables and toss to coat. Remove the rice from the oven and serve the sweet and sour chicken (or pork) over the rice.

TACOS

Serves 4

This taco meat is also good served over rice instead of in tortillas, and it freezes well.

2 medium tomatoes, chopped
½ small onion, chopped
4 leaves Romaine lettuce, cut in thin shreds
salsa
2 cups shredded dairy or non-dairy cheese
1 Tbsp. oil
1 lb. of one of the following: ground beef or turkey; beef round steak or pork cutlets, cut in strips; or boneless chicken, cut in strips
1 Tbsp. chili powder
2 tsp. cumin
¼ tsp. cayenne pepper (optional)
½ tsp. onion powder
½ tsp. garlic salt (or plain salt)

1 tsp. paprika

½ tsp. lemon pepper (or black pepper plus a little squeeze of lemon juice)

½ tsp. Mexican oregano

8–12 tortillas (made with corn, spelt, all-purpose flour, or rice flour)

oil for frying corn tortillas (no oil is needed for spelt, all-purpose flour, or rice tortillas)

plus salsa, avocado, black olives, refried beans, sour cream or Ranch Dressing (see p. 125), etc.

Put the tomatoes, onion, lettuce, cheese, and salsa into separate serving bowls and set them aside.

Heat 1 Tbsp. oil in a nonstick pan over medium-high heat and fry the meat and all the spices together until the meat is tender. Transfer the meat to a serving bowl and keep warm.

If you are serving the tacos with corn tortillas, wipe out the frying pan and add a scant tablespoon of oil. Fry the corn tortillas one-by-one on both sides until they are soft and pliable. Stack them on a serving plate and keep them covered with a towel to keep them warm.

If you are using non-corn tortillas, lay a hand towel over the tortilla serving plate to wrap hot tortillas in so they will stay warm until serving time. Heat a cast iron or nonstick frying pan over medium-high heat (no oil is needed). Put one or two tortillas in the pan at a time and heat them on each side until they are hot, about 1 minute per tortilla. As the tortillas finish heating, start stacking them on top of each other, keeping them covered with the towel, until all heated tortillas are together in one stack. They will keep each other very warm under the towel. Serve them hot.

Let each person assemble their own tacos by arranging the meat and other condiments in tortillas.

Cook the pasta according to the package directions. Pour the pasta into a colander, rinse it with cool water, and set it aside to drain.

Measure all the remaining ingredients into a two-quart saucepan. Heat the sauce over medium heat and allow it to simmer for 5 minutes. Add the pasta to the tomato sauce and toss to coat. Cook the pasta in the sauce until it is heated through before transferring it to a serving dish.

CARROT MASHED POTATOES

Serves 4

2 baking potatoes (1 ¼ pounds), peeled and cut into 1-inch pieces
3 carrots (¾ lb.), cut in ½ inch pieces
¼ cup dairy or non-dairy milk
¼ cup salted butter, dairy-free margarine, or coconut oil
½ tsp. salt
black pepper, to taste

Pour enough water into a medium-sized saucepot to come ½ inch up the sides of the pan. Put the potato and carrot pieces into the pot and cover it with the lid. Turn the heat to high. As soon as the water comes to a boil, turn the heat down to medium and set a timer for 15 minutes. Do not remove lid while cooking.

When the timer goes off, check the potatoes and carrots to see if they are tender. When they're ready, drain off the water. Then add the milk, butter, salt, and pepper. Mash the vegetables using a potato masher or an electric mixer until they are smooth and creamy.

SPANISH RICE

Serves 4

Serve this tasty and moist rice with tacos or as a side dish to any main meat course.

¼ cup safflower oil or other oil of choice
1 clove garlic, minced
½ cup yellow onion, finely chopped
1 ½ cups basmati or jasmine rice or other rice of choice

1 tsp. cumin seed

⅛ tsp. black pepper

¼ tsp. salt

14.5 oz. diced tomatoes

2 ½ cups chicken broth or water

In a medium-sized saucepot, heat the oil over medium heat. Add the garlic and onion. Sauté the mixture, stirring occasionally, about 7 minutes or until the onions are tender.

Meanwhile, put the rice in a strainer and run cold tap water over it for about 20 seconds, massaging the rice to loosen all the starch. Let the rice drain until onions are done.

When the onions are tender, add the cumin, pepper, and salt. Cook for about 1 minute, then add the rice and sauté the mixture, continually scraping the pan, until the rice is lightly browned. Add the tomatoes and broth. Stir the rice to be sure it isn't sticking to the bottom of the pot. Put a lid on the pot. When it starts boiling, turn it down to low and simmer the liquid for about 20 minutes until the rice is done. (Cook brown rice for 40–45 minutes.) Do not remove the lid or stir the rice while it is cooking. At the end of the cooking time, check to see if rice is done by skimming off a few of the top grains of rice with a fork. It is ready when the top grains are tender. If rice is not done after cooking 20 minutes, add an 2 additional tablespoons of water, cover the pot with the lid, and cook for 5 minutes longer.

To serve, press the cooked rice into a small cereal bowl and invert the rice onto a plate.

PART EIGHT

SAUCES AND CONDIMENTS

BARBECUE SAUCE

Makes about 2 cups sauce

This sauce takes only 10 minutes to make.

8 oz. tomato sauce
6 oz. tomato paste
⅜ cup brown sugar
¼ cup apple cider vinegar
¼ tsp. garlic powder
¾ tsp. onion powder
½ tsp. dry mustard
½ tsp. chili powder
⅜ tsp. cayenne pepper
½ tsp. allspice
⅛ tsp. black pepper
½ tsp. mesquite liquid smoke
½ tsp. Worcestershire sauce
1 tsp. salt

OIL AND VINEGAR DRESSING

Makes 3 cups

1 ¾ cups olive oil
1 ¼ cup red wine vinegar
¾ tsp. black pepper
2 ½ tsp. salt
1 tsp. Italian seasoning
1 clove garlic, finely minced

Put all the ingredients into medium-sized mixing bowl. Whisk the liquid until everything is blended. Let the dressing sit on the counter for a few minutes until the flavor develops, then whisk the dressing again at serving time.

STRAWBERRY SAUCE

Makes about 3 cups

Berry sauces are good served over ice cream, angel food cake, or on pancakes. They freeze well for up to three months.

1 quart strawberries (about 1 ½ lbs.)
scant ½ cup granulated sugar

Wash and hull the strawberries and allow them to drain in a colander. Pulse the berries in a food processor or place them in a bowl and use a potato masher to crush them. Add the sugar and stir the strawberries until the sugar has dissolved. Transfer the strawberry sauce to a refrigerator storage container. Cover the sauce and allow it to chill in the refrigerator until serving time.

BERRY SAUCE

Makes about 3 cups, depending on what kind of berry is used

4 cups blueberries, raspberries, blackberries, huckleberries or Marion
      berries, or a mixture of several kinds of these berries
½ cup granulated sugar

2 Tbsp. cornstarch or tapioca flour
1–2 tsp. lemon juice

Place all the ingredients in a medium-sized saucepan and bring the mixture to a boil over medium heat, stirring occasionally. Once it boils, turn the heat to low and simmer the sauce for 2 minutes, stirring occasionally. Cool the sauce and pour it into a covered storage container. Allow it to chill in the refrigerator.

Note:

When making these sauces, the granulated sugar may be replaced with any sugar substitute of choice.

FUDGE SAUCE

Makes about 3 ½ cups sauce

Store-bought fudge sauce steps aside for this homemade version! I adapted my grandpa's old tried-and-true fudge sauce recipe to come up with this allergy-friendly version, which freezes well when made with hemp or rice milk.

1 ⅔ cups dairy or non-dairy milk
2 cups granulated sugar

10 Tbsp. baking cocoa
2 Tbsp. canola oil
1 tsp. vanilla

Measure the milk into a heavy two-and-one-half-quart saucepan.

In a separate bowl, mix the sugar and cocoa together; whisk the dry mixture into the milk. Stir in the oil and put the saucepan on the stove, uncovered, over medium heat. Whisk until all the ingredients are blended. Bring the sauce to a boil, whisking every so often but never scraping the sides of the pan.

As soon as the mixture comes to a boil, turn the heat down to low. Set the timer for 15 minutes and continue cooking the sauce uncovered. Whisk it every so often, but do not touch the sides of the pan while it is cooking or it may form hard sugar crystals. At the end of 15 minutes, remove the pan from heat. Stir in the vanilla.

The sauce will thicken as it cools. Place the saucepan on a potholder and let it sit for 15 minutes without stirring. After 15 minutes, beat the sauce with a wooden spoon for 2 minutes, scraping down the sides and bottom of the pan. Serve the sauce warm or cold and store the leftovers in a covered container in the refrigerator for up to 2 weeks (if it lasts that long).

CARAMEL SAUCE

Makes about 3 cups sauce

This sauce makes a great ice cream topping!

¼ cup canola oil or other oil of choice
2 cups brown sugar
⅔ cup dairy or non-dairy milk
½ cup brown rice syrup or white corn syrup
scant ⅛ salt
¼ cup salted butter, dairy-free margarine, or coconut oil

Measure all the ingredients except butter into a heavy two-quart saucepan with a thick bottom. Put the saucepan on the stove over medium heat. Stir to blend the ingredients.

Bring the sauce to boil over medium heat. Once it starts boiling, turn the heat to low and simmer for 2 minutes, stirring occasionally but not scraping the sides of the pan. Remove the pan from the heat and stir in the butter. Let the sauce cool to room temperature.

WHITE SAUCE

Makes about 2 cups sauce

This is the sauce I use in this cookbook as the basis for cream sauces for pasta and vegetable dishes. It freezes excellently when made with hemp or rice milk.

2 cups dairy or non-dairy milk
choose one of the following: 2 Tbsp. cornstarch, potato starch, or tapioca
    flour (gluten-free); ¼ cup spelt flour (wheat-free, but not gluten-free); or
    ¼ cup all-purpose or whole wheat flour (contains wheat and gluten)
½ tsp. salt

¼ tsp. black pepper
2 Tbsp. salted butter, dairy-free margarine, or oil of choice

Measure the milk, flour, salt, and pepper into one-quart saucepan and whisk the ingredients together. Put the saucepan on the stove over medium heat. Whisk the liquid occasionally until it comes to a boil and thickens. Remove the pan from the heat. Add the butter and whisk the sauce until the butter has melted.

The quantities given make a medium-thick sauce, but you may adjust the thickness of the sauce by adding more or less flour. If the sauce is too thick, thin it by adding more milk, 1 teaspoon at a time. For a thicker sauce, increase the flour by 1–2 tablespoons.

Variations
- **Caraway sauce:** Add 1 tsp. caraway seeds along with the butter.
- **White wine sauce:** Substitute ¼ cup cooking sherry for ¼ cup milk.

CHEESE-FREE CHEESE SAUCE

Makes about 2 cups cheese-free sauce

one recipe White Sauce (above)
½ cup nutritional flake yeast
½ tsp. dry mustard
¼–½ tsp. turmeric (optional, for pretty yellow color)

Follow the directions for the white sauce, adding the flake yeast and dry mustard when the flour is added. Whisk in enough turmeric to produce the desired color of yellow.

HONEY BUTTER

Makes about 1 ½ cups

1 cup salted butter or dairy-free margarine, at room temperature
½ cup honey

Measure all the ingredients into a small mixing bowl and beat them together with a spoon until well blended. Place the butter in the refrigerator to chill until serving time.

Variation
- **Maple cinnamon honey butter:** Replace ¼ cup of the honey with ¼ cup pure maple syrup. Add 1 Tbsp. ground cinnamon.

1 tsp. oregano
1 qt. (4 cups) vegetable stock
2 cups water
1 lb. lentils (about 2 ¼ cups)
14.5 oz. stewed tomatoes or 1 pound fresh chopped tomatoes
salt and black pepper to taste

Heat the oil in a Dutch oven or medium-sized soup pot over medium heat. Sauté the celery, onions, and carrots for 2 minutes. Add the meat and cook the mixture for another 5–7 minutes or until meat is done. Sprinkle the spices over the meat at the end of the cooking time and stir to make the spices fragrant. Add all the remaining ingredients and cover the soup with a lid. Bring the liquid to a boil over medium heat, then turn down the heat and allow the soup to simmer for 1 hour, stirring occasionally, until the lentils are done.

CARROT-RAISIN SALAD

Makes 2 cups (four ½-cup servings)

2 cups peeled and grated carrots
   (about ½ lb. carrots)
⅔ cup raisins
3 Tbsp. mayonnaise or vegan
   mayonnaise

Mix together the carrots, raisins, and mayonnaise. Serve within 4 hours for maximum freshness.

COLESLAW

Serves 5-6

Making coleslaw with vegan mayonnaise makes it "heart-healthy," as well as dairy-free and egg-free.

16 oz. coleslaw mix greens (or 7 ½ cups shredded cabbage and carrots)

½ cup mayonnaise or vegan mayonnaise
2 Tbsp. cider vinegar
2 Tbsp. granulated sugar
¼ tsp. salt
pepper
½–2 tsp. celery seed (to taste)
¼–½ tsp. xanthan gum to thicken dressing (optional)

Transfer the coleslaw mix to a large mixing bowl. Mix all the remaining ingredients together in a small bowl and stir them together. (If you like the dressing even thicker, whisk in ¼ tsp. xanthan gum.) Pour the dressing over the coleslaw and toss the salad to coat it evenly in the dressing. Transfer the coleslaw to a serving bowl and cover it with plastic wrap. This salad needs to chill in the refrigerator for at least 2–3 hours for the flavors to develop.

CHICKEN SALAD SANDWICHES

Makes 3 ½ cups chicken salad

This recipe is also good when made with tuna fish. Using soy-, dairy-, and egg-free mayonnaise makes it allergy-friendly.

1 ½ cups (12.5 oz.) shredded cooked
  chicken (or tuna fish)
2 Tbsp. finely chopped onion
2 Tbsp. finely chopped celery
2 Tbsp. grated carrot
¼ cup mayonnaise or vegan mayonnaise
salt and pepper to taste
Gluten-Free Sandwich Rolls (see p. 27), or bread of choice
Lettuce, tomatoes, onions, pickles, etc.

In a medium-sized mixing bowl, combine the chicken, onion, celery, carrot, mayonnaise, salt, and pepper. Put a slightly heaping ⅓ cup of chicken salad on four different sandwich rolls. Garnish the sandwiches with lettuce, tomatoes, onions, pickles, and olives.

POTATO SALAD

Serves 6-8

This recipe is good with or
without eggs.

3 lbs. red potatoes (or potato of
   choice), peeled and cut in ½-inch
   cubes
4 ½ Tbsp. vinegar, or dill pickle juice
2 tsp. salt, divided
½ cup pickle relish, or finely
   chopped dill pickles
¾ cup chopped celery or ¾ tsp. celery seed
¾ cup yellow onion, chopped fine
3 hard-boiled eggs, cooled, peeled, and chopped small (optional)
¼ tsp. black pepper
¾ cup mayonnaise or vegan mayonnaise
2–3 Tbsp. mustard (to taste)

To steam the potatoes, fill a three-quart saucepot with ½ inch water. Add the potatoes and sprinkle them with 1 tsp. salt. Cover the pot with a snugly fitting lid. Bring the water to a boil over high heat. Turn the heat to low and simmer the liquid for 10–15 minutes without removing lid until the potatoes are done. Drain the potatoes in a colander.

Transfer drained potatoes to a four-quart mixing bowl and drizzle them with vinegar. Toss the potatoes to ensure they are evenly coated and allow them to cool comletely. Add the pickle relish, celery, onion, and chopped eggs and mix the ingredients together.

In a separate small bowl, mix 1 tsp. salt, pepper, mayonnaise, and mustard. Pour the dressing over the potatoes and toss the salad to coat the ingredients evenly. Cover the salad and chill it until serving time.

THREE-BEAN SALAD

Serves 6

The oil dressing in this salad is very light, which is the way I like it. Those who like their salad swimming in dressing need to double the dressing recipe!

Salad
14.5 oz. green beans, drained
15 oz. red kidney beans, drained (about 1 ¾ cups)
15 oz.garbanzo beans, drained (about 1 ¾ cups)
½ cup red onion, chopped
Black olives and parsley to garnish (optional)

Dressing
⅓ cup cider vinegar
¼ cup olive oil
2 tsp. granulated sugar
1 tsp. Dijon mayonnaise
¼ tsp. Italian seasoning
½ tsp. salt
Black pepper to taste

In a medium-sized serving bowl, toss the drained beans and onions together.

Whisk the dressing ingredients together and pour them over the beans. Toss the ingredients to coat them evenly in the dressing.

Cover the bowl with plastic wrap and marinate the salad in the refrigerator for at least 2–3 hours or overnight. Every so often the salad ingredients need to be turned over to ensure that the dressing is distributed equally over all the beans. Each time the salad is turned in its bowl, put the plastic wrap back over the top and return the salad to the refrigerator.

This salad is best when it is prepared the day before it will be served.

PART TEN

VEGETABLE SIDE DISHES

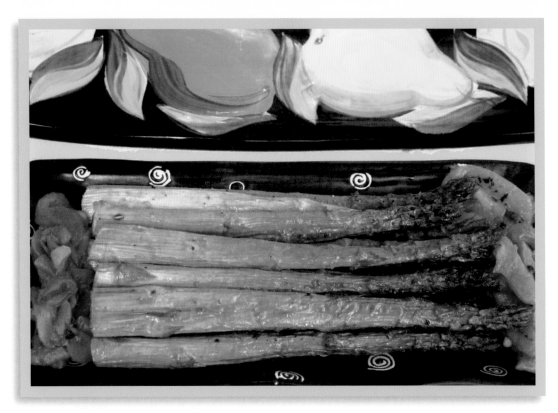

OVEN ROASTED ASPARAGUS WITH LEMON DILL DRESSING

Serves 4

This recipe works with almost any vegetable. One batch of the dressing is enough for any one of the vegetables listed below.

Lemon dill dressing:
   4 tsp. olive oil
   ½ tsp. sugar
   1 tsp. rice vinegar
   1 tsp. lemon juice
   ½ tsp. lemon pepper
   ½ tsp. salt
   2 tsp. dill

Choose one of the vegetables in this list:

1 ¾ lbs. asparagus, washed and tough ends removed (results in 1 lb. trimmed spears)

1 lb. baby carrots

1 lb. zucchini or yellow squash, cut in ¼-inch thick strips

1 lb. broccoli or cauliflower, cut into flowerets

1 onion, peeled and cut in ¼-inch slices

1 head celery, trimmed and cut into sticks

1 lb. mushrooms, whole or cut in half

2 bell peppers, seeded and cut into ½-inch strips

Preheat the oven to 400°.

In a 9- x 13-inch pan, measure all the ingredients for the dressing, mixing them with a fork. Put the asparagus (or other vegetables) in the pan and stir them with a fork to coat all the sides in the dressing.

Put the pan in the oven and set a timer for 10 minutes. After the asparagus has cooked for 10 minutes, remove the pan from the oven and lightly shake the pan to turn the asparagus over. Return the pan to the oven for an additional 10 minutes.

When the vegetables are tender, serve them immediately.

Variations of dressings to coat vegetables with:

- **Italian dressing:** 4 tsp. olive oil, ½ tsp. sugar, 1 tsp. rice vinegar, ½ tsp. garlic salt, and 2 tsp. Italian seasoning
- **Mustard dressing:** 4 tsp. olive oil, 1 ½ tsp. prepared mustard, 1 tsp. sugar, 1 tsp. rice vinegar, ¼ tsp. garlic salt, and ¼ tsp. black pepper

STIR-FRIED GREEN BEANS AND BELL PEPPERS

Serves 4

I lived in Hong Kong for five years, and during that time I learned to cook a few Chinese dishes. No one taught me to make this one, but after being around that wonderful Chinese style of cooking, I just applied what I learned to these green beans. The result? Delicious!

1 ¼ lbs. fresh green beans, with the ends removed (frozen may be used,
    but will not produce a true tender-crisp texture)
½ red or yellow bell pepper, seeded and cut into thin strips
2 cloves garlic, minced (optional)
2 Tbsp. canola oil or other oil of choice
1 Tbsp. sesame oil (or more canola)
2–3 Tbsp. soy sauce or fish sauce, to taste (the sauces may be replaced
    with salt, to taste)

Measure the canola oil into a medium-sized nonstick frying pan and set the heat on medium-high. When the oil is hot, add the green beans, bell pepper, and garlic. Stir-fry the vegetables for 3 minutes, then turn the heat to medium-low and put a snugly fitting lid on the pan. For tender-crisp vegetables, steam them for 10 minutes, stirring every 2 minutes or so. For vegetables that are thoroughly cooked and soft, steam them 15 minutes.

Just before serving, splash the vegetables with 1 Tbsp. sesame oil and 2 Tbsp. soy sauce and add black pepper to taste. Add more soy sauce, if desired.

Yams in Orange-Sherry Glaze

Serves 4-5

At Thanksgiving and Christmas, this is one of my favorite dishes.

3 lbs. yams (or sweet potatoes)
½ cup frozen orange juice
    concentrate, thawed
⅓ cup cooking sherry
½ cup brown sugar
2 Tbsp. salted butter or dairy-free
    margarine, melted

Preheat the oven to 350°.

Place the yams, whole, in a two-quart casserole dish with a snugly fitting lid. Add 2 Tbsp. water and microwave the yams on high for 10 minutes. Let the yams steam in the casserole dish for another 5 minutes.

When they are cool to the touch, remove the yam skins and cut them into 1-inch thick slices. Arrange the slices in a 9- x 13-inch baking pan. Sprinkle the yams lightly with salt.

start to wilt. Turn the heat to medium before adding the green onions. Allow the vegetables to cook until they are tender, about 6–8 minutes.

Variation

- **Potato cauliflower curry:** Omit 2 cups of the cabbage. When the spices are added in step 2, add 3 cups peeled potatoes, quartered and then cut into ¼-inch slices. Cook the vegetables for 8–10 minutes or until the potatoes start to brown. Then add the cauliflower, carrots, and green onions, and sauté the vegetables until the cauliflower is tender, about 12–14 minutes.

Appendix

WHERE TO PURCHASE
ALLERGY-FRIENDLY INGREDIENTS

Allergy-friendly products are always being added to the market, updated, and changed. Please check the Web sites of each of the companies below to see a new list of products being offered and to see pictures of their products. From time to time, products are reformulated and ingredients may change. Therefore, be sure to read the labels *each time* you purchase a product to confirm that all the ingredients are compatible with your specific food allergies.

The products listed in this appendix are available in grocery or health food stores, or may be ordered online.

COMPANY NAME	PRODUCTS AVAILABLE
Bob's Red Mill 13521 SE Pheasant Court Milwaukie, OR 97222 (503) 654-3215 Mail Order: (800) 349-2173 Fax: (503) 653-1339 www.bobsredmill.com/home.php	Every kind of flour, starch, and grain used in this cookbook, as well as gluten-free oatmeal and xanthan gum, are available through Bob's Red Mill.
Chicago Soydairy PO Box 666 Glen Ellyn, IL 60138-0666 (630) 629-9667 www.chicagosoydairy.com/index/php	They provide a dairy-free soy cheese that melts easily and a soft-serve dairy-free ice cream with a rich, creamy texture.
Enjoy Life Foods 3810 N. River Road Schiller Park, IL 60176 (888) 50-ENJOY www.enjoylifefoods.com	Enjoy Life Foods sells gluten-free, dairy-free, and soy-free products, like chocolate chips and ready-made cookies, cereals, and snacks.

COMPANY NAME	PRODUCTS AVAILABLE
Follow Your Heart Foods/Earth Island PO Box 9400 Canoga Park, CA 91309 (818) 725-2820 www.followyourheart.com info@followyourheart.com	Their products—like an egg-free mayonnaise called Vegenaise®, sour cream, cream cheese, and several different kinds of cheeses—are gluten-free, egg-free, and dairy-free but contain soy products.
Galaxy Nutritional Foods, Inc. 5955 T. G. Lee Blvd, Suite 201 Orlando, FL 32822 (800) 441-9419 Ext. 224 www.galaxyfoods.com/default.asp www.EatGreenforBodyandEarth.com	Galaxy Nutritional Foods, Inc., provides cheese made three ways: soy-free and casein-free, soy-free but containing casein, and containing both soy and casein. Their cheeses are sold sliced, in blocks, and grated.
Earth Balance® is a trademark and registered trademark of GFA Brands, Inc. (201) 568-9300 www.earthbalancenatural.com	These natural and organic products contain soy. Many products are dairy-free and contain heart-healthy omega-3's, such as their natural buttery spreads (non-dairy margarine) and non-hydrogenated vegan shortening.
The Hain Celestial Group, Inc., offers several brands of allergy-free products: Arrowhead Mills®: www.arrowheadmills.com DeBoles®: www.deboles.com WestSoy®: www.westoy.biz Dream®: www.tastethedream.com Spectrum®: www.spectrumorganics.com The company's main Web site is www.glutenfreechoices.com.	They provide many different kinds of gluten-free flour; organic, gluten-free pastas; rice and soy beverages; rice, soy, and almond milk, as well as ice cream; non-hydrogenated, soy-free shortening; egg-free, dairy-free, and soy-free mayonnaise; salad dressings of many flavors (read labels); many flavors of mayonnaise (read labels)
Seelect Herb Tea Company 1145 W. Shelly Court Orange, CA 92868 (714) 771-3317 www.seelecttea.com	This company offers organic flavoring oils and extracts and natural, gluten-free food coloring. Read the labels of each product.

COMPANY NAME	PRODUCTS AVAILABLE
Oregon® Fruit Products Co. PO Box 5283 Salem, OR 97304 1-800-394-9433 www.oregonfruit.com	Oregon Fruit Products Co. provides canned fruits and berries from the northwest. Some are packed in water, some in a light syrup, and some in heavy syrup. All their ingredients are natural, their fruit contains no preservatives, and the flavor is exceptional.
Breads from Anna Gluten Evolution, LLC 4172 Alyssa Court Suite A Iowa City, IA 522476 (319) 354-3886 www.breadsfromanna.com	Breads from Anna provides certified kosher foods. She has many gluten-free bread mixes. Anna told me she can find almost any allergy-free ingredient a person may need. I found her while looking for lemon and orange rind that contain no food dye. Call her at the number to the left, and she will be happy to assist you in finding allergy-free ingredients you need.

TO CONTACT THE AUTHOR

susan.gauen@charter.net

www.celebratingfoodglutenfree.com